KU-863-406

Guide to
Reflexology
and Complementary Therapies

BROCKHAMPTON PRESS
LONDON

This edition published 1996 by Brockhampton Press,
a member of the Hodder Headline PLC Group

ISBN 1 86019 311 0

Printed and bound in India

Contents

Reflexology

Introduction

Reflexology is a technique of diagnosis and treatment in which certain areas of the body, particularly the feet, are massaged to alleviate pain or other symptoms in the organs of the body. It is thought to have originated about five thousand years ago in China and was also used by the ancient Egyptians. It was introduced to Western society by Dr William Fitzgerald, who was an ear, nose and throat consultant in America. He applied ten zones (or energy channels) to the surface of the body, hence the term 'zone therapy', and these zones, or channels, were considered to be paths along which flowed a person's vital energy, or 'energy force'. The zones ended at the hands and feet. Thus, when pain was experienced in one part of the body, it could be relieved by applying pressure elsewhere in the body, within the same zone.

Subsequent practitioners of reflexology have concentrated primarily on the feet, although the working of reflexes throughout the body can be employed to beneficial effect.

Reflexology does not use any sort of medication—merely a specific type of massage at the correct locations on the body. The body's energy flow is thought to follow certain routes, connecting every organ and gland with an ending or pressure point on the feet, hands or another part of the body. When the available routes are blocked, and a tenderness on the body points to such a closure, then it indicates some ailment or condition in the body that may be somewhere other than the tender area. The massaging of particular reflex points enables these channels to be cleared, restoring the energy flow and at the same time healing any damage.

The uses of reflexology are numerous, and it is especially effective for the relief of pain (back pain, headaches and toothache), treatment of digestive disorders, stress and tension, colds and influenza, asthma, arthritis, and more. It is also possible to predict a potential illness and either give preventive therapy or suggest that specialist advice be sought. The massaging action of reflexology creates a soothing effect that enhances blood flow, to the overall benefit of the whole body. Reflexology, however, clearly cannot be used to treat conditions that require surgery.

Reflex massage initiates a soothing effect to bring muscular and nervous relief. The pressure of a finger applied to a particular point (or nerve ending) may create a sensation elsewhere in the body, indicating the connection or flow between the two points. This is the basis of reflexology, and although pain may not be alleviated immediately, continued massage over periods of up to one hour will usually have a beneficial effect.

There are certain conditions for which reflexology is inappropriate, including diabetes, some heart disorders, osteoporosis, disorders of the thyroid gland, and phlebitis (inflammation of the veins). It may also not be suitable for pregnant women or anyone suffering from arthritis of the feet.

The best way to undergo reflexology is in the hands of a therapist, who will usually massage all reflex areas, concentrating on any tender areas that will correspond to a part of the body that is ailing. Reflexology can, however, be undertaken at home on minor conditions such as back pain, headache, etc, but care should be taken not to over-massage any one reflex point as it may result in an unpleasant feeling. Although there have not been any clinical trials to ascertain the efficacy of reflexology, it is generally thought that it does little harm and, indeed, much benefit may result.

Some practitioners believe that stimulation of the reflex points leads to the release of endorphins (in a manner similar to acupuncture). Endorphins are compounds that occur in the brain and have pain-relieving qualities similar to those of morphine. They are derived from a substance in the pituitary gland and are involved in endocrine control (glands producing hormones, for example, the pancreas, thyroid, ovary and testis).

The Reflexes

Reflexes on the hands and feet
Reflexes on the feet—the soles of the feet contain a large number of zones, or reflexes, that connect with organs,

glands or nerves in the body, as shown in figures 1 and 2 on pages 13 and 14. In addition, there are a small number of reflexes on the top of the foot, as shown in figures 10A and B on page 42.

The *palms of the hands* similarly contain a large number of reflex areas, reflecting to a very large extent the arrangement seen on the soles of the feet, as shown in figures 3 and 4 on pages 15 and 16. The backs of the hands again mirror, to some extent, the tops of the feet, containing a smaller number of reflex areas (*see* figure 11 on page 59).

Use of the hands in reflexology

The hands are considered to have an electrical property, so that the right-hand palm is positive and the left-hand palm is negative. In addition, the right hand has a reinforcing, stimulating effect while the left has a calming, sedative effect. The back of each hand is opposite to the palm, thus the right is negative and the left is positive. This is important when using reflexology because if the object is to revitalize the body and restore the energy flow that has been limited by a blockage then the right hand is likely to be more effective. The left hand, with its calming effect, is best used to stop pain.

Reflexes on the body

Reflexes on the body necessarily differ from those on the feet and hands in that there is less alignment with the ten zones (figures 5 and 6 on pages 18 and 19 show some of the reflexes). Also, there are a number of reflex points on

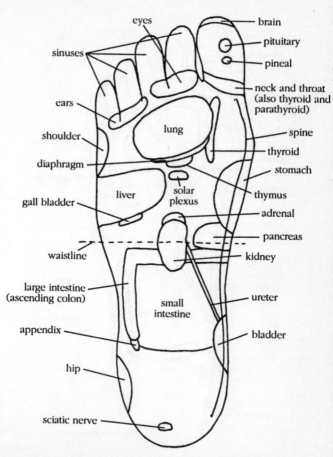

figure 1: major reflex points on the sole of the right foot

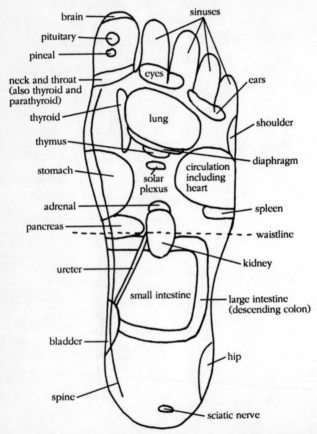

figure 2: major reflex points on the sole of the left foot

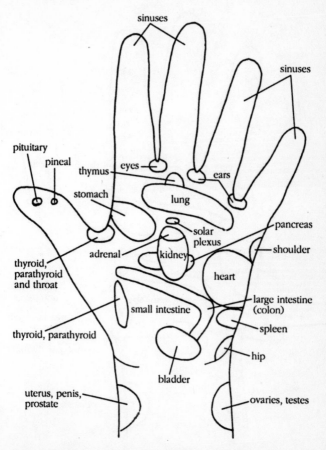

figure 3: major reflex points on the palm of the left hand

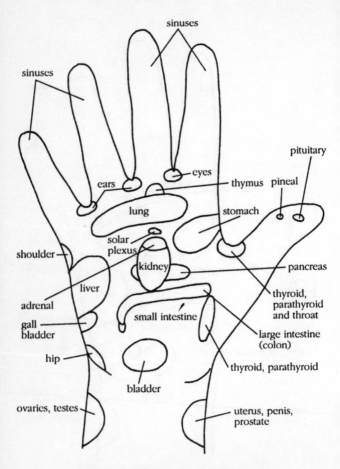

*figure 4: major reflex points on the
palm of the right hand*

the body that correspond to several organs or glands. These reflex points are sometimes harder to find accurately and may be more difficult to massage.

The middle finger is thought to have the greatest effect, so this should be used to work the reflex point. Light pressure should be applied to each point, and if pain is felt it means there is a blockage or congestion somewhere. A painful point should be pressed until the discomfort subsides or for a few seconds at a time, a shorter rest being taken in between the applications of pressure.

The abdominal reflex

A general test can be applied by gently pressing into the navel, either with the middle finger or with one or both hands, with the individual lying in a supine position. The presence of a pulse or beat is taken to mean there is a problem in this area. To combat this, the same technique is used, holding for a few seconds (six or seven), releasing slightly, and keeping the fingers in the same area, gently massaging with a circular action. If it is necessary to press quite deep to feel the beat, then heavier massage will be required to provide the necessary stimulation.

The same principle can be applied to other reflex points in the abdominal region, and the absence of a pulse or beat indicates that there is no problem. In each case, should there be a painful response, holding for a few seconds invokes the sedative action.

Chest reflexes

There are a number of reflex points on the chest relating to

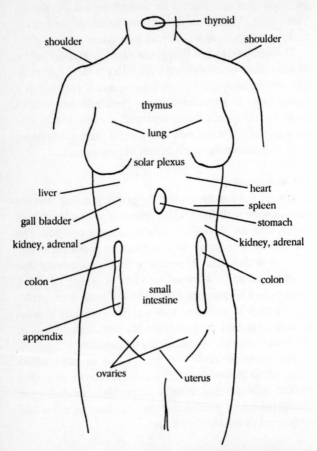

figure 5: major reflexes on the body (female)

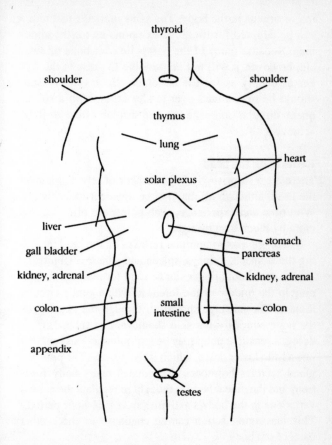

figure 6: major reflex areas on the body (male)

major organs in the body. The same massage technique can be adopted for these reflex points as for the abdomen. Because many of the points lie over bone or muscle, however, it will not be possible to press in the finger as deeply as for the abdomen. However, pressure should be maintained over tender areas, with a subsequent circular massage, and a similar effect will be achieved.

Reflexes on the head

There are a surprisingly large number of reflex points on the head, although all may not be apparent immediately. With time and experience, such points are often located more by touch than by sight.

There are many important reflexes on the head including the stomach, kidneys, spleen and pancreas (figure 7). Again, the middle finger can be used for massage, beginning in the middle of the forehead with a gentle circular motion. The massage should go through the skin to rub the bone beneath—the skin should not be rubbed. In so doing, a sensitive point may be felt (pituitary) and another one a little lower down, which is the pineal. (The pituitary gland secretes hormones that control many body functions and the pineal body is thought to regulate the natural variations in the body's activities over a 24-hour period.) This massaging action can be continued to check other parts of the body.

The back of the head also shows a large number of reflexes. However, there are a number of ways of stimulating the body as a whole through the head. These include:

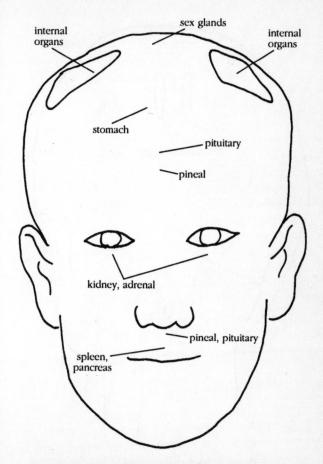

figure 7: some of the major reflex points on the head

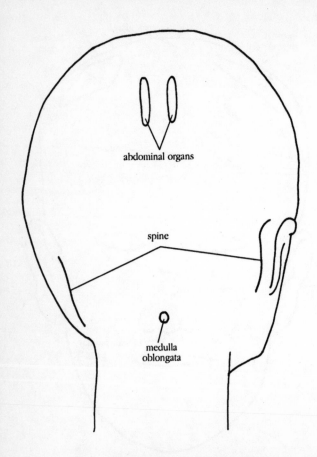

*figure 8: back of the head to show the
medulla oblongata reflex*

1 tapping the head gently with the fists, all over and
   very quickly for a period of about thirty seconds
2 pulling handfuls of hair
3 tapping the head gently with a wire brush

Each has a specific result, for example, stimulating the hair,
but also enlivening organs and glands over the whole body.

One particularly important reflex point is the medulla
oblongata (figure 8). The medulla oblongata is the lowest
part of the brain stem, which joins to the upper part of the
spinal cord. It contains important centres for the control of
respiration, swallowing, salivation and the circulation.
This reflex point is located at the nape of the neck, towards the base of the skull. Massage of this point opens
all channels within the body and generates a vitality, relieving nervous tension and producing almost instant energy. The point should be pressed and massaged to produce the desired effects.

Ear reflexes
The ear has long been used in acupuncture because, in addition to its ease of use, it contains scores of acupoints,
which correspond to the reflex points in reflexology.
Some of these points are shown in figure 9 on page 24.

The ear is perhaps the most difficult area of the body to
work with because there are so many reflexes in such a
small space. It becomes essentially a question of touch,
pressing and exploring, and any sore point located can be
massaged and worked out. By using a gentle squeeze-and-
roll method on the tops of the ears and the ear lobes a

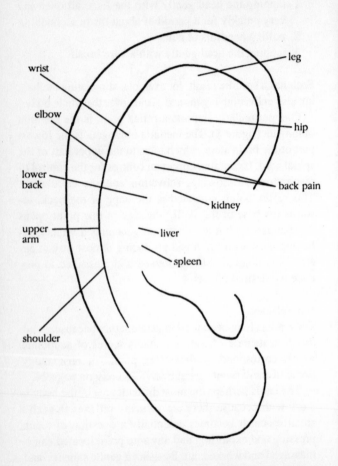

figure 9: some of the major reflex points on the ear

number of areas can be stimulated. It has been reported
that reflexology can help ear problems such as ringing in
the ears, and the condition tinnitus may be alleviated to
some extent.

Techniques and Practice

Some indication of the massaging, manipulative procedures of reflexology have already been mentioned, but a
number of general points of guidance can also be made.

The whole process of reflexology is one of calm, gentle
movements in a relaxed state. The foot is probably used
most in reflexology, in which case shoes and socks and
stockings, etc, should be removed. A comfortable position
should be adopted on the floor or bed, in a warm, quiet
room with the back supported by pillows.

To begin, the whole foot is massaged, indeed both feet
should ideally be worked on. However, if working on
your own feet it is thought that the right foot should be
massaged first (contrary to previous practice). It is considered that the right foot is linked with the past, hence
these emotions must be released before the present and
future aspects are dealt with in the left foot.

Techniques of massage vary, but a simple method with
which to start involves placing the thumb in the middle of
the sole of the foot. The thumb then presses with a circular
and rocking motion for a few seconds before moving to
another reflex. Reference can be made to the diagrams to
determine which reflex is being massaged. In all cases,

the massage should work beneath the skin, not on the skin. Another method involves starting the massage with the big toe and then moving on to each toe in turn. In using the thumbs to effect the massage, some refinements of motion can be introduced to give slightly different movements.

1 The thumb can be rocked between the tip and the ball, moving forwards over the relevant area. This, along with the circular massage already mentioned, relieves aches and pains.
2 Both thumbs can be used alternately to stroke the skin firmly. This creates a calming effect.
3 The area can be stroked with the thumbs, one moving over the other in a rotational sense. This action is intended to soothe and allow for personal development.

In addition to the procedures already mentioned, reflexology can be used to alleviate many symptoms and help numerous conditions. The following sections provide examples of these uses. Reflexology can be approached intuitively, so that the pressure of touch and the time factor can vary depending upon response and need.

The Use of Reflexology

The digestive system

The *stomach* is an organ that has thick muscular walls and in which food is reduced to an acidic semi-liquid by the action of gastric juices. There are many factors that can cause an upset stomach. To assess the general condition, the stomach body reflex (above the navel) can be pressed. Around it are several related reflexes such as the liver, gall bladder, intestines and colon. The reflex should be pressed for a few seconds and then released three times to activate the reflex.

On the *hands*, the web of soft tissue between the thumb and forefinger of the left hand should be worked with the thumb of the right hand for a few minutes. The hands can be reversed but the stronger effect will be gained this way, because the stomach lies mostly on the left side.

On the *feet*, the reflexes for the stomach are found primarily on the instep of the left foot, although they are also present on the right foot. These should be massaged, but there are further factors, in addition to the use of reflexology, that will aid digestion. These include eating a sensible diet with a minimum of artificial substances, and not overeating. The use of certain essential oils (aromatherapy) can also be of benefit. In this case peppermint oil can often be particularly effective.

The *colon* is the main part of the large intestine in which water and salts are removed from the food that enters from the small intestine. After extraction of the water, the waste remains are passed on to the rectum as faeces. If this system becomes unbalanced in any way, then the water may not be absorbed or the food remains pass through the colon so quickly that water cannot be absorbed. In such cases, the result is diarrhoea, which can be painful and inconvenient.

Both body and foot reflexes should be massaged for

the stomach, intestines, colon and also the liver and kidneys. The thyroid reflex should also be worked to help regulation of the body functions. A useful body reflex is to press and rotate your finger about two inches above the navel for a couple of minutes. This can be repeated numerous times, each time moving the fingers a little clockwise around the navel until a complete circuit has been made.

It is important that the condition be stabilized as soon as possible as continued loss also leads to loss of vital salts and a general nutritional deficiency.

At the outset it is possible to work the colon reflexes on the hand to identify any tender areas. The right thumb should be pressed into the edge of the pad (around the base and side of the thumb) of the left palm and worked around to seek out any tender spots. Any tender reflex should be massaged and pressed for a few seconds. In each case, the tenderness should be worked out. Since there are many reflex points crowded onto the navel, it may not solely be the colon reflex that requires some attention. It is always useful to work the reflex on both sides of the body to ensure a balance is achieved.

A similar approach can be adopted for reflexes on the feet, starting at the centre, or waistline. By applying a rolling pressure, the foot is massaged along to the inner edge and then down the line of the spine and any tender points are worked through pressure and massage. It may be necessary to start with a very light pressure if the area is very tender, and then as the soreness lessens, the pressure can be increased.

Again, diet can be an important factor in maintaining the

health of the body and the workings of the colon. Fibre is particularly important in ensuring a healthy digestive system and avoiding ailments such as diverticulitis.

Reflexology can be used for other conditions associated with the digestive system, notably ulcers. A peptic ulcer (in the stomach, duodenum or even the oesophagus) is caused by a break in the mucosal lining. This may be due to the action of acid, bile or enzymes because of unusually high concentrations or a deficiency in the systems that normally protect the mucosa. The result can be a burning sensation, belching and nausea.

To help alleviate the problem, which may often be stress-related, the reflexes in the feet should be massaged, as these are often the most relaxing. Obviously, the important reflexes are the stomach and duodenum, but it is also worthwhile to work on the liver and the endocrine glands (notably the pituitary). If the ulcer is a long-standing problem or if stomach complaints have been experienced for some time, then further medical help is probably needed.

The heart and circulatory system
The heart is obviously a vital organ. This muscular pump is situated between the lungs and slightly left of the midline. It projects forward and lies beneath the fifth rib. Blood returns from the body via the veins and enters the right atrium (the upper chamber), which contracts, forcing the blood into the right ventricle. From there it goes to the lungs where it gains oxygen and releases carbon dioxide before passing to the left atrium and left ventricle. Oxy-

genated blood then travels throughout the body via the arteries.

By using body reflexes, the heart can be maintained, and conditions can be dealt with by massaging the appropriate reflex points. A useful massage exercise is to work the muscles, rather than the reflex points, of the left arm in a side-to-side movement. This can be followed by the neck muscles and the chest muscles; in each case any tightness or tension should be massaged out. An additional preventive is a good diet, which should be low in fat and food high in cholesterol, but should contain adequate amounts of vitamins, notably the B group, C and E. Exercise is, of course, very important to maintain a good heart and circulation.

There is also a simple test that many reflexologists feel is useful in the diagnosis of possible heart problems. It may also be worth doing if strenuous activity is contemplated in the near future. Pressure is applied to the pad of the left thumb, at the top. The pressure should be quite hard. It is suggested that when this part of the pad hurts, it indicates a constriction in blood vessels, limiting supply. If the bottom of the pad hurts, this is indicative of congested arteries. If the area is too tender to touch (and there is no physical damage to the hand) then there is a possibility of a heart attack. This test thus provides advance warning and enables a medical doctor to be consulted. Should painful areas occur on both hands, this does *not* indicate a heart problem.

Many blood and circulatory disorders will benefit from the same sort of massage. In these cases the foot reflexes for the endocrine glands (hypothalamus, pituitary, pineal, thyroid and parathyroid, thymus, adrenals, pancreas, ovary or testis) should be worked well, as should those for the circulatory system and heart, lungs and lymphatic system.

Conditions that may benefit from such treatment include:

angina
a suffocating, choking pain usually referring to angina pectoris, which is felt in the chest. It occurs when blood supply to the heart muscle is inadequate and is brought on by exercise and relieved by rest. The coronary arteries may be damaged by atheroma (scarring and buildup of fatty deposits). Of particular importance are the heart and circulatory reflexes (veins and arteries) and those of the lymphatic system.

arteriosclerosis
a general term including atheroma and atherosclerosis (where arteries degenerate and fat deposits reduce blood flow), which results generally in high blood pressure and can lead to angina. Additional reflexes that should be worked include the liver.

hypertension (high blood pressure)
this may be one of several types, the commonest being *essential* (due to kidney or endocrine disease or an unknown cause) and *malignant* (a serious condition that tends to occur in the younger age groups). In addition to the re-

flexes for the blood and circulation, those for the shoulders, neck and eyes should be worked, in combination with reflexes for the digestive system and liver.

palpitations

an irregular heartbeat, often associated with heightened emotions. Also due to heart disease or may be felt during pregnancy. The lung and heart reflexes are particularly important, in addition to those of the circulation.

Some heart conditions are very serious and require immediate hospitalization, e.g. cardiac arrest (when the heart stops) and coronary thrombosis (a coronary artery blockage causing severe chest pain, vomiting, nausea and breathing difficulties. The affected heart muscle dies, a condition known as myocardial infarction). However, massage of appropriate reflexes may help, particularly in less serious cases. These should include the heart and circulation (veins and arteries), lungs, endocrine system and the brain. Each will have some beneficial effect in relieving stress and congestion.

varicose veins

veins that have become stretched, twisted and distended, and this often happens to the superficial veins in the legs. The possible causes are numerous and include pregnancy, defective valves, obesity and thrombophlebitis (the inflammation of the wall of a vein with secondary thrombosis). Phlebitis is inflammation of a vein and occurs primarily as a complication of varicose veins. Both these conditions can be treated by massaging the circulatory reflexes and also the leg and liver reflexes. In both cases, resting with the legs in an elevated position is beneficial.

The respiratory system

Asthma is one of the major problems of the respiratory system and its incidence seems to be escalating. The condition is caused by a narrowing of the airways in the lungs. It usually begins in early childhood and may be brought on by exposure to allergens (substances, usually proteins, that cause allergic reactions) exercise or stress.

There are certain body reflexes that can help in this instance. One reflex point is in the lower neck at the base of the V-shape created by the collar bones. Relief may be achieved by pressing the finger into this point with a downward motion for a few seconds. There are additional reflex points on the back, at either side of the spine in the general region of the shoulder blades. These can be worked by someone else with thumb or finger, who should press for a few seconds. Other reflexes that can be worked on the foot include the brain, endocrine glands such as the pineal, pituitary, thymus and thyroid, the lungs, and also the circulatory system. Particular attention should be paid to the lungs, which includes the bronchi and bronchioles, the branching passageways of the lungs where gaseous exchange (oxygen in, carbon dioxide out) takes place. At the point where the instep meets the hard balls of the feet, and along the base of the lung reflex area is the massage point for the diaphragm. Working the whole of this area will help alleviate symptoms of asthma. During an attack of asthma, both thumbs can be placed on

the solar plexus reflexes immediately to initiate the soothing process.

The adrenal glands are found one to each kidney, situated on the upper surface of that organ. These are important endocrine glands because they produce hormones
such as adrenaline and cortisone. Adrenaline is very important in controlling the rate of respiration and it is used
medically in the treatment of bronchial asthma because it
relaxes the airways. It is clear therefore, that the adrenal is
an important reflex and it is located in the middle of each
sole and palm.

Many other respiratory disorders can be helped by using massage of the same reflexes: brain, endocrine glands,
lungs and diaphragm, neck and shoulders, augmented by
the heart and circulatory system. Conditions responding
to this regime include bronchitis, croup, lung disorders
and emphysema (distension and thinning, particularly of
lung tissue, leading to air-filled spaces that do not contribute to the respiratory process).

Infections of the respiratory tract leading to coughs and
colds can also be helped primarily by working the reflexes
mentioned above. For colds, the facial reflexes should be
massaged, especially that for the nose. However, it is
good practice to include the pituitary, and to work the in-
dex and middle fingers towards the tip to help alleviate
the condition.

With such respiratory problems, there are complementary therapies that can help such as homoeopathy,
aromatherapy and Bach flower remedies. There are also
many simple actions that can be taken, for example a sore

throat may be helped by gargling regularly with a dessert-spoon of cider apple vinegar in a glass of water, with just a little being swallowed each time. Honey is also a good substance to take, as are onion and garlic.

The endocrine glands

Endocrine glands are glands that release hormones directly into the bloodstream, or lymphatic system. Some organs, such as the pancreas, also release secretions via ducts. The major endocrine glands are, in addition to the pancreas, the thyroid, parathyroid, pituitary, pineal, thymus, adrenal and gonads (ovaries and testes).

The endocrine glands are of vital importance in regulating body functions as summarized below:

pituitary	controls growth, gonads, kidneys; known as the master gland
pineal	controls the natural daily rhythms of the body
thyroid	regulates metabolism and growth
parathyroid	controls calcium and phosphorus metabolism
thymus	vital in the immune system, particularly pre-puberty
adrenal	control of heartbeat, respiration and metabolism
gonads	control of reproductive activity
pancreas	control of blood sugar levels

The fact that the endocrine glands are responsible for the very core of body functions means that any imbalance should be corrected immediately to restore the normality. There are some general points relating to massage of these reflex areas. It is good practice to massage the brain reflex first and then the pituitary. This is because the hypothalamus, situated in the forebrain, controls secretions from the pituitary gland. The pituitary gland then follows as this is the most important in the endocrine system. The reflexes should be gently massaged with thumb or finger for a few seconds and then gentle pressure exerted and held for a few seconds before releasing slowly.

The pituitary

An imbalance of pituitary gland secretions, often caused by a benign tumour, can lead to acromegaly (excessive growth of skeletal and soft tissue). Gigantism can result if it occurs during adolescence. There may also be consequent deficiencies in adrenal, gonad and thyroid activity. The brain and endocrine reflexes should be worked in order, supplemented by those for the circulation, liver and digestion. In addition to reflex points on the hands and feet, there is also one on the forehead. If any of these reflex areas is found to be tender, it should be massaged often to maintain the balance necessary for healthy growth.

The pineal

The pineal body, or gland, is situated on the upper part of the mid-brain, although its function is not fully understood. It would seem, however, to be involved in the daily rhythms of the body and may also play a part in controlling sexual activity. The pineal reflex points are found close to those of the pituitary on the big toes, thumbs and on the forehead and upper lip.

The thyroid
The thyroid is located at the base of the neck and it produces two important hormones, thyroxine and triiodothyronine. Under or overactivity of the thyroid leads to specific conditions.

If the thyroid is overactive and secretes too much thyroxine (hyperthyroidism), the condition called thyrotoxicosis develops. It is also known as Grave's disease and is typified by an enlarged gland, protruding eyes and symptoms of excess metabolism such as tremor, hyperactivity, rapid heart rate, breathlessness, etc. The important reflexes on which to concentrate are the brain and solar plexus, endocrine system and also the circulatory and digestive systems. The reflexes are found on the soles and palms and using the thumbs or fingers, the areas should be massaged, but in stages if the area is very tender.

Underactivity of the thyroid, or hypothyroidism, can cause myxoedema producing dry, coarse skin, mental impairment, muscle pain and other symptoms. In children a similar lack causes cretinism, resulting in dwarfism and mental retardation. The reflexes to be worked are essentially those mentioned for hyperthyroidism, and in addition (for both conditions) the liver reflexes on the right sole and palm should benefit from attention.

There are additional thyroid reflexes elsewhere on the body, notably on the neck roughly midway between jaw and collarbone and on either side. These points should be massaged gently with the thumb and fingers on opposite sides of the throat. Using a gentle gyratory motion, the massage can be taken down to the collarbone, the fingers and thumb of the other hand are then used (on opposite sides of the throat) and the procedure repeated.

Goitre is another condition associated with the thyroid and is a swelling of the neck caused by enlargement of the gland, typically due to overactivity of the gland to compensate for an iodine deficiency. The important reflexes to concentrate upon are the brain, solar plexus, endocrine system and circulatory system but working of all body reflexes will help.

The parathyroid

There are four small parathyroid glands located behind or within the thyroid. They control the use of calcium and phosphorus (as phosphate) in the body's metabolism. An imbalance of these vital elements can lead to tetany (muscular spasms), or at the other extreme, calcium may be transferred from the bones to the blood, creating a tendency to bone fractures and breaks.

The reflexes to these glands are found in the same location as those for the thyroid but it will probably be necessary to massage more strongly to achieve an effect. It is a good idea to work on these areas each time reflexology is undertaken as they are vital in maintaining the metabolic equilibrium of the body.

The thymus

The thymus is located in the neck (over the breastbone) and is a vital contributor to the immune system. It is larger in children and is important in the development of the immune response. After puberty it shrinks although seems to become more active later in life. Bone marrow cells mature within the thymus and one group, T-lymphocytes, are dependent upon the presence of the thymus. These are important cells as they produce antibodies.

The commonest disorder associated with the thymus is myasthenia gravis, which lowers the level of acetylcholine (a neurotransmitter) resulting in a weakening of skeletal muscles and those used for breathing, swallowing, etc. The thymus reflexes are found on the soles of the feet and palms of the hand, next to the lung reflexes. The thymus can also be stimulated by tapping with the finger over its position in the middle of the upper chest.

The adrenals
The two adrenals (also known as suprarenals) are situated one above each kidney and consist of an inner medulla and an outer cortex. The medulla produces adrenaline, which increases the rate and depth of respiration, raises the heartbeat and improves muscle performance, with a parallel increase in output of sugar from the liver into the blood.

The cortex of the adrenal glands releases hormones including aldosterone, which controls the balance of electrolytes in the body, and cortisone, which, among other functions, is vital in the response to stress, inflammation and fat deposition in the body.

On both the palms and soles, the adrenal reflexes are located above those for the kidneys and if this area is at all tender, it should be massaged for a few seconds. Because the kidney and adrenal reflexes are close together, the massage should be limited to avoid over-stimulation of the kidney reflexes. Disorders of the adrenal glands should be treated by working the endocrine reflexes starting with the pituitary and including the adrenal reflexes themselves, followed by the reflexes for the circulatory, liver and urinary systems.

Specific disorders include Cushing's syndrome, caused by an overproduction of cortisone, which results in obesity, reddening of the face and neck, growth of body and facial hair, high blood pressure, osteoporosis and possibly mental disturbances, and Addison's disease, which results from damage to the cortex and therefore a deficiency in hormone secretion. The latter was commonly caused by tuberculosis but is now due more to disturbances in the immune system. The symptoms are weakness, wasting, low blood pressure and dark pigmentation of the skin. Both these conditions can be treated by hormone replacement therapy but reflexology can assist, through massage of the endocrine, digestive and liver reflexes.

The gonads
The gonads, or sex glands, comprise the ovaries in women and testes in men. The ovaries produce eggs and also secrete hormones, mainly oestrogen and progesterone. Similarly, the testes produce sperm and the hormone testosterone. Oestrogen controls the female secondary sexual characteristics such as enlargement of the breasts, growth of pubic hair and deposition of body fat. Proges-

terone is vital in pregnancy as it prepares the uterus for implantation of the egg cell.

The reflexes for these and related organs are found near the ankles on the inside of the feet, just below the angular bone (*see* figure 10 on page 42). The same reflex areas are also located on the arms, near the wrist. The ovaries and testes are on the outer edge, while on the opposite, inner edge, are the reflexes for the uterus, penis and prostate.

For any disorders that might involve the ovaries or testes, it is also useful to massage other systems such as the brain, other endocrine glands, the circulation and liver.

The pancreas
This is an important gland with both endocrine and exocrine functions. It is located behind the stomach, between the duodenum and spleen. The exocrine function involves secretion of pancreatic juice via ducts, into the intestine. The endocrine function is vital in balancing blood sugar levels through the secretion of two hormones, insulin and glucagon. Insulin controls the uptake of glucose by body cells and a lack of hormone results in the sugar derived from food being excreted in the urine, the condition known as diabetes mellitus. Glucagon works in the opposite sense to insulin, and increases the supply of blood sugar through the breakdown of glycogen in the liver, to produce glucose.

The primary reflexes for the pancreas are found on the soles and palms, near to the stomach. The thumb should be used, starting on the left foot, working across the reflex area and on to the right foot. If the area is tender, it should

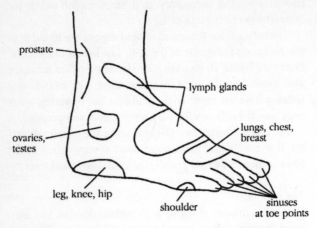

figure 10A: reflex areas on the outside of the foot

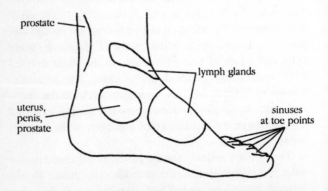

figure 10B: reflex areas on the inside of the foot

be worked until the tenderness goes. Because there are numerous reflexes in this area, there will be stimulation of other organs, to the general wellbeing of the body as a whole.

For other disorders of the pancreas, such as pancreatitis (inflammation of the pancreas) the reflexes associated with digestion should also be worked. Pancreatitis may result from gallstones or alcoholism and, if sufficiently severe, may cause diabetes.

The liver and spleen

The liver is a very important organ and is critical in regulating metabolic processes. It is the largest gland in the body and is situated in the top right hand part of the abdominal cavity. Among the functions, the liver converts excess glucose to glycogen, which is stored as a food reserve; excess amounts of amino acids are converted into urea for excretion; bile is produced for storage in the gall bladder and some poisons are broken down. The liver also recycles red blood cells to remove the iron when the cells reach the end of their life; it stores vitamins and produces blood clotting substances. Due to its high chemical and biochemical activity, the liver generates a lot of heat and is the major contributor of heat to the body.

The reflex area for the liver is a large area, reflecting the size of the organ, on the right palm and right sole, on the outer edge. As a general procedure, the area should be massaged with the left thumb, searching for tender points. More massage may be required for the liver than for other reflexes.

Hepatitis is inflammation of the liver due to viral infection or the presence of toxins. Alcohol abuse commonly causes hepatitis, and it may also be due to drug overdose or drug side effects. Viral infections such as HIV and glandular fever can also cause hepatitis. There are several types of hepatitis, designated A to E, and all may persist in the blood for a long time.

To combat such disorders, after removing the source of any toxins, the reflex for the liver and digestion should be worked and the reflexes for the eyes. Dietary restraint is also important and should involve natural foods with little or no alcohol, caffeine, nicotine and a low intake of fats.

Associated with the liver, anatomically, is the gall bladder. This is a small sac-like organ that stores and concentrates bile. When fats are digested, the gall bladder contracts, sending bile into the duodenum. Sometimes stones form here, and often gallstones can cause severe pain. The gall bladder reflex is found at the foot of the liver on the right palm and foot. On the body there is another reflex just below the ribs on the right-hand side, and below the liver reflex point. A steady pressure should be held around the point, beginning near the navel and working to the right side, maintaining pressure for a few seconds on any tender point.

The spleen is situated on the left side of the body behind and below the stomach. The spleen produces leucocytes (white blood cells), lymphocytes (a white blood cell involved in the immune system), blood platelets (involved in blood coagulation) and plasma cells. It also acts as a store for red blood cells, which are made available in emergencies (when oxygen demand is greater).

The reflex area for the spleen is found on the left palm or sole, below the reflex for the heart. If a tender point is found in this reflex, it may indicate anaemia and it would then be wise to obtain a blood test.

The kidneys and bladder

The reflexes for the kidneys are found just off centre on the palms of both hands and soles of both feet. They are close to the pancreas and stomach. The bladder reflex is towards the base of the palm, near the wrist and on the feet it is found on the inside edge of both soles, towards the heel. There are also body reflexes for both organs.

The kidneys are important organs in the body's excretory system. They are responsible for processing the blood continuously to remove nitrogenous wastes (mainly urea) and they also adjust salt concentrations. By testing the reflexes with the thumb, tender areas can be located and worked upon. However, prolonged massage should be avoided—it is better to use shorter periods of 15–20 seconds initially as the system becomes accustomed to the treatment.

The body reflexes for the kidney are at the side of the body, almost at the waistline, between the hip and rib cage. They also occur on the face, just beneath the eyes.

It is not surprising, considering the pivotal role of the kidneys in removing body wastes, that any interference with their normal function can lead to serious illnesses. General kidney disorders, kidney stones, nephritis and pyelitis are all best aided by massaging the kidney reflex but also the reflexes for the central nervous system, the endocrine glands (especially the pituitary and adrenal glands), liver, stomach and circulation. Kidney stones are formed by the deposition of solid substances that are naturally found in the urine but that precipitate out for one reason or another. They are commonly salts of calcium, and the alteration in pH of the urine is often a contributory factor. Nephritis is inflammation of the kidney and pyelitis is when part of the kidney, the pelvis, becomes inflamed. If the whole kidney becomes affected, it is then called pyelonephritis.

Disorders associated with the bladder tend to be infections such as cystitis or other physical manifestation of a problem whether through stress or a medical condition. The latter category includes enuresis (bed-wetting) and incontinence. In these cases, the bladder reflex should obviously be worked upon, and the reflexes for the brain, solar plexus and endocrine system.

The alleviation of back pain and other skeletal disorders
Within the working population of most countries, back pain accounts for millions of days in lost production. This is not unexpected as the spine is the primary part of the skeleton, hence any problem with it will inevitably upset the body and its overall wellbeing.

On the soles of the feet, the reflex for the spine is located along the inner edge of both feet running from the base of the big toe almost to the heel. By working this line with the fingers, any tender points can be found and worked upon. The top end of the line, near the toe, is equivalent to the spine at the level of the shoulders.

With back disorders, such as lumbago, additional reflexes should be worked including the brain and endocrine system. Because the body's musculature is a complementary and antagonistic system with the skeleton,
creating all the movements of which the body is capable,
the muscles are also important when dealing with back
pain. It will help therefore to massage muscles, rubbing quite
deeply with the fingers, and moving across the muscles.

Back pain can result from a problem elsewhere in the
body with posture, tight muscles or even flat feet. It is important to be aware of the possibilities and ensure that the
treatment deals with the problem as a whole, and not just
in part. Exercise is clearly beneficial and walking can help
loosen and strengthen muscles associated with the back. A
brisk walk is fine, but jogging is not necessarily the best
remedy, as in some cases this can itself prove harmful.

Reflexologists often turn to the muscles in the legs to
alleviate back pain, particularly in the area of the lower
back. The muscles at the back of the thigh should be massaged with a pressing and pulling action, first with one
hand and then the other. The whole of the thigh should be
treated, from the top of the leg, to the knee. Massage of
both legs in this manner, concentrating on any 'tight' areas, will help improve the overall tone and assist in elimi-
nating causes of back pain.

Study of the diagrams for the feet and hands reveals
specific reflex areas for the shoulders, hip and neck.
When working on skeletal disorders in general, it is wise
to undertake a thorough massage of specific reflex areas
such as neck and shoulders, plus those for the brain, solar

plexus, the endocrine system, remainder of the skeletal system, endocrine glands, etc. For particular conditions such as bursitis (inflammation of a joint, as in housemaid's knee), general joint pain, stiff neck and similar complaints, a common regime of reflexological massage applies. This should include working the skeletal reflexes along with those for the nervous and endocrine system, digestive and circulatory systems. It is usually the case that the specific complaint will benefit from massage of its reflex area and most of those that comprise a whole body workout. It should always be remembered that there are occasions when surgery may prove essential, e.g. in the case of a hip replacement.

The knee joint can often be the source of pain and discomfort. It may help to apply gentle pressure on either side of the knee, just where the bone ends, using the thumb and middle finger. This should be held for a few seconds, pressing as much as possible (do not press hard if it is too painful) and then the same should be done below the knee.

Relief from arthritis with reflexology
Arthritis can be a crippling disease and many people suffer from it. It is an inflammation of joints or the spine, the symptoms of which are pain and swelling, restriction of movement, redness and warmth of the skin. Two forms of the condition are osteoarthritis and rheumatoid arthritis.

Osteoarthritis
Osteoarthritis involves the cartilage in joints, which then

affects the associated bone. What often happens is that the cartilage is lost, to be replaced by osteophytes at the edges of the bones. These are bony projections that occur with the loss of cartilage or with age. The projections affect the joint function, causing pain.

Rhematoid arthritis
Rheumatoid arthritis is the second commonest joint disease after osteoarthritis. It usually affects the feet, ankles, wrists and fingers in which there is a swelling of the joint and inflammation of the synovial membrane (the membraneous envelope around the joint). Then follows erosion and loss of cartilage and loss of bone. At its worst, the condition can be disabling.

Massage of the reflex areas for the affected areas should be worked but, as mentioned previously, it is important to massage the reflexes for the whole body to achieve a complete and balanced approach. The endocrine system is one important system in this respect.

In seeking ways to treat rheumatoid arthritis, the medical profession isolated the glucocorticosteroid hormone, cortisone, from the adrenal glands of cattle. It was found that the use of cortisone had dramatic effects on the symptoms of rheumatoid arthritis. However, the relief was only temporary, and an additional disadvantage was the occurrence of associated side effects, which could be severe, e.g. damage to muscle, bone, stomach ulcers, bleeding and imbalances in the hormonal and nervous systems. The medical use of this compound is therefore very restricted, but it is produced naturally by the adrenal cortex. Being a natural secretion, there are no detrimental side effects. There is a reflex point in the lower back, between the first and second lumbar vertebrae, which can be pressed. Finding this point will be hit and miss initially, but upon locating it (roughly 5 centimetres up from the coccyx or tailbone), apply gentle pressure, gradually increasing, and hold it for a few seconds. This should be repeated several times. This is helpful for other conditions, in addition to rheumatoid arthritis, such as asthma and bursitis.

As with back disorders, muscle condition is also felt to be important in the treatment of arthritis. The muscles in the area affected by arthritis should be massaged by pressing in with the fingers, either on or near to the area. The massage should be across the muscles, with a deep motion, although it may initially produce discomfort or soreness. Many practitioners regard this as an important supplementary technique in administering reflexology.

Stress and tension

One of the additional beneficial effects of reflexology when dealing with a particular reflex area or point is that the treatment is very relaxing. If most of the body reflexes are massaged, a feeling of wellbeing is generated, and tension is released. Stress control and relief can be accomplished in a number of ways, some of which happen instinctively, such as deep breathing and, paradoxically, wringing the hands. The latter is an obvious way of working the reflex points, albeit that it is mostly done unconsciously. A related method of calming the nerves is to intertwine the fingers, as in clasping the hands, which enables all the reflexes between the fingers to be pressed. This should be done several times. Deep breathing is a common method of relaxation that ultimately can envelop the whole body, providing that the focus of attention is the attainment of the correct pattern of breathing. Mental attitude is also an important aspect of reflexology. It clearly makes sense, while undergoing massage (with or without a practitioner or partner) to imagine, or listen to, pleasing sounds, rather than worrying about the pressures of modern life. If there is no access to relaxing sounds (bird song, running water, etc) it is perfectly possible to imagine it, and thereby to augment the physical relaxation with mental calm.

The *endocrine glands* are considered important in combating stress because they are responsible for the hormonal balance of the body. All reflex areas for these glands, on both soles and palms, should be massaged and special attention given to the thyroid, which controls body temperature and can help restore calm. The adrenal reflex point, almost in the centre of the hand, is also important, and, because it is so near the solar plexus, receives equal attention. (The solar plexus is a network of nerves and ganglia in the sympathetic nervous system concerned with body functions not under conscious control. It is located behind the stomach).

Quite often stress and tension can result in a sore neck or back. A number of reflex points can be worked to relieve these sorts of complaint. The medulla oblongata is important in this respect as it controls some major body functions such as the circulation. The point on the back of the head (*see* figure 8 on page 22) should be held with the middle finger for a few seconds and then released, and repeated several times. The reflex points of the spine should also be worked starting at the neck reflex, which is found below the base of the big toe or thumb. By moving down the side of the foot, the whole spine can be covered. To relieve a sore back completely and effectively, other reflexes to be attended to should include the shoulders, hips, and the sciatic nerve. The sciatic nerve is made up of a number of nerve roots from the lower part of the spinal cord, and pain with this origin may be felt in the back of the thigh, buttock and the foot. The reflex point may at first be painful to the touch, but through careful massage it can be worked to assist in promoting relief.

Control of the heart rate is a natural, complementary procedure in promoting stress relief. If a situation, wherever it may be, results in you feeling stressed, massaging the reflex areas for the heart will help, whether on foot or hand.

Sound, restful sleep is refreshing and also contributes to a reduction in stress. Reflexology can also help in this respect through the feeling of relaxation that it induces. The clasping of the hands, mentioned earlier, can be used to combat sleeplessness. The fingers can be clasped on the chest and then worked over each other so that the length of each finger is massaged. The fingers should remain intertwined and simply be released a little to allow each finger over the first knuckle, when the fingers are squeezed together again. This, associated with deep breathing will encourage relaxation.

Reflexology and the reproductive system

The major reflexes of the reproductive system are those for the uterus, ovary and breast in the female, and the penis, testes and prostate in the male. The ovary reflexes are found on the outer side of the foot, just below the ankle (*see* figure 10). On the hand, these are found a little way beyond the wrist (*see* figures 3 and 4), on the outer edge. On both foot and hand, the breast reflex is found on the outer edge, a little below the base of the little toe or finger. The uterus reflex on the hand occupies a position opposite to the ovaries, i.e. just below the wrist, but on the inner edge of the arm. On the foot, this reflex mirrors that for the ovary, but it is on the inside of the foot, below the ankle.

The male reflexes

The male reflexes occupy the same positions as those of the female, thus the penis reflex is in the same position as that for the uterus and the testes is the same as the ovaries. The prostate gland reflexes are situated with the penis reflex and also at the back of the leg/foot, above the heel, (*see* figure 10, page 42).

There are also reflex points on the head for the gonads (*see* sex glands on figure 7, page 21). As well as working the various reflexes for the reproductive system, it is beneficial to pay attention to the endocrine gland reflexes as they have considerable control over the gonads (*see* endocrine glands, page 35). In particular, the pituitary, thyroid and adrenal glands and their hormonal secretions have a large influence on the reproductive system. All these points should be massaged to stimulate activity and ensure that hormone secretion is balanced and gonad activity is normal. The body reflexes can also be used to this end by pressing each point for a few seconds and repeating several times for all endocrine and sex glands.

If any of the endocrine glands are tender, it may be indicating a problem with the sex glands. By working the various reflex points, it is possible to ensure a healthy reproductive system. There are a number of reflexes to the penis and testes that can help in this respect. The sex reflex below the navel should be pressed with fingers or thumb and massaged for a few seconds. Additional reflex points on the legs, about 15 centimetres above the ankle on the inside of the leg, should also be massaged. Initially, massage here should be for half a minute or so, because any problems will make it tender. However, with further attention it will be possible to work out the soreness. A further point on the leg lies above the knee, in the soft area on the outer edge, above the kneecap. All these reflexes, if worked in turn, will contribute to a healthy system and lead to fewer problems, such as impotence.

Impotence itself can, however, be treated. In addition to undertaking the massage of reflex points and areas mentioned above, there are further techniques that may help. There is a particularly sensitive and stimulating area between the anus and scrotum, which should be pressed gently a number of times. It is also said that if gentle on-off pressure is applied to the scrotum, this will help.

Another problem faced by many men involves the prostate gland. This gland is situated below the bladder and opens into the urethra, which is the duct carrying urine out of the body and which also forms the ejaculatory duct. On ejaculation, the gland secretes an alkaline fluid into the sperm to help sperm motility. In older men particularly, the prostate gland may have become enlarged, causing problems with urination. Working the appropriate reflexes may help this situation as may massaging the base of the penis. However, it is advisable to check with a medical doctor to ensure that there is no other condition present.

The female reflexes
There are a number of female conditions that may be helped by reflexology. In most cases, the reflexes to be worked are very similar and the following complaints are therefore grouped in this way:

amenorrhoea lack of menstruation, other than during pregnancy or pre-puberty

endometriosis the occurrence of endometrial cells, normally found in the womb, elsewhere in the body, e.g. Fallopian tubes or peritoneum, causing pain and bleeding

fibroid a benign tumour of the uterus that may cause pain, bleeding and urine retention

leucorrhoea discharge of white/yellow mucus from the vagina, which may be normal before and after menstruation, but at other times large amounts signify an infection

dysmenorrhoea painful menstruation

menorrhagia excessive blood flow during menstruation

For these and related conditions, the general procedure should be to spend time on the specific female reflex, which in these cases is the uterus. In addition the endocrine gland reflexes should be massaged and to provide a balanced treatment, the reflexes for the other reproductive organs (ovary, etc) should be worked. Further areas to concentrate upon include the urinary and circulatory systems and the central nervous system (brain) with the solar plexus.

Premenstrual tension (or syndrome) is the condition typified by headache, nervousness, irritability, depression and tiredness (in addition to physical symptoms) several days before the start of menstruation. It is advisable, before menstruation starts, to have a thorough massage of the reflexes once or twice per week. Next, the reflexes for the uterus and ovaries should be worked. The uterus reflex is on the inside of the foot in the soft area beneath the ankle. The massage should work all around the ankle, beginning with a gentle pressure, and then working back towards the heel. The other foot should then be dealt with in the same way.

To help overcome depression the endocrine glands are very important to regulate hormones, maintain body rhythms and balance the biochemical functions—all of which have some effect on emotions. Other reflexes to work, in addition to the endocrine glands, include the solar plexus, brain and liver. The liver is very important in this respect and, although the area should not be over-worked, it should not be forgotten.

The *menopause* is the time when a woman's ovaries no longer release an egg cell every month, and child-bearing is no longer possible. This usually occurs between the ages of 45 and 55. It may be preceded by a gradual decline in the frequency of menstruation or there may be an abrupt cessation. There is an imbalance in the sex hormones and this can cause a number of symptoms, including hot flushes, sweats, palpitations, depression and vaginal dryness. Over a longer period there may be a gradual loss of bone (osteoporosis) leading to a greater risk of bone fractures.

In this instance, the endocrine reflexes are once again very important. In conjunction with these, the reflexes for the spine and brain should be worked, the former to promote relaxation. As a general point, the reflexes to the spine can be massaged for any length of time whereas those for organs and glands should be worked periodically and for a few seconds each time.

To help combat hot flushes, the thyroid reflex should be worked since this is the endocrine gland responsible for the control of the metabolic rate. Regulation of breathing through deep breaths will also help.

The breasts are, of course, the mammary glands that produce milk at the appropriate time, but in today's society they have also become important from a cosmetic point of view. Disorders of the breasts can include lumps or cysts, pain or tenderness. Such conditions may be due to an hormonal imbalance but in any event will benefit from a complete treatment of all the reflexes on feet, hands or head. The breast reflex is found on the top of the foot or hand, at the base of the toes or fingers, and this should be worked regularly. Since the endocrine system is of great significance in the reproductive system, all glands reflexes should receive some attention. Reflexological massage can also be used as a general technique to maintain healthy breasts. Essentially the hand should form a cup around the breast with the fingers underneath and the nipple between thumb and forefinger. Using a circular movement the breast is massaged slightly upwards. This should help retain the shape of the breast, and maintain its tone.

Diseases of the immune system

The human body resists infection by means of antibodies and white blood cells. Antibodies are protein substances produced by the lymphoid tissue (spleen, thymus gland and the lymph nodes) that circulate in the blood. They react with their corresponding antigens (foreign bodies that cause antibodies to be formed) and make them harmless. There are a number of immunoglobulins (large protein molecules) that act as antibodies, and each has a particular function. For example, one is responsible for allergic reactions and another is produced to fight bacteria and viruses in the body.

The lymphatic system is also important in the body's immune response. Lymph nodes are swellings that occur at various points in the system. They are found in the neck, groin and armpit, and their main function is to re-

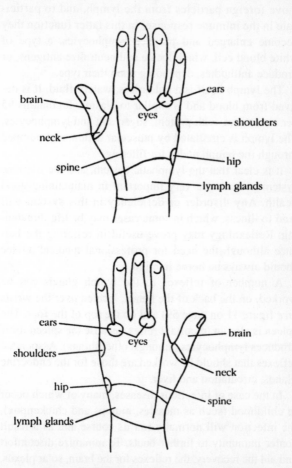

figure 11: reflexes on the backs of the hands

move foreign particles from the lymph, and to participate in the immune response. In this latter function they become enlarged and produce lymphocytes, a type of white blood cell, which locate and neutralize antigens, or produce antibodies, depending upon their type.

The lymph itself is a colourless, watery fluid. It is derived from blood and is similar to plasma. It contains 95 per cent water, with protein, sugar, salt and lymphocytes. The lymph is circulated by muscular action, and pumped through the lymph nodes for filtering.

It is clear that the lymphatic system, and the immune system overall, are very important in maintaining good health. Any disorder or deficiency in this system will lead to illness, which in some cases may be life-threatening. Reflexology may prove useful in restoring the balance although the need for professional medical advice should always be borne in mind.

A number of reflexes to the lymph glands can be worked, on the back of the hands, located over the wrists (*see* figure 11 on page 59) and on the top of the foot. The spleen is also an important reflex because the spleen itself produces lymphocytes (amongst other things). Associated reflexes that should be worked are those for the endocrine glands, circulation and liver.

In the case of infectious diseases, many of which occur in childhood (such as measles, mumps and chickenpox), the infection will normally run its course and as a result confer immunity to further bouts. To minimize discomfort and aid the recovery, the reflexes for the brain, solar plexus, circulation, endocrine glands and liver should be massaged.

The same applies to most infectious conditions, even autoimmune diseases where the antibodies attack their own body cells. In these cases, the lymph gland reflexes are particularly important.

Shiatsu

Introduction

Shiatsu originated in China at least 2000 years ago, when the earliest accounts gave the causes of ailments and the remedies that could be effected through a change of diet and way of life. The use of massage and acupuncture was also recommended. The Japanese also practised this massage, after it had been introduced into their country, and it was known as *anma*. The therapy that is known today as *shiatsu* has gradually evolved with time from anma under influences from both East and West. It is only very recently that it has gained recognition and popularity, with people becoming aware of its existence and benefits.

Although East and West have different viewpoints on health and life, these can complement one another. The Eastern belief is of a primary flow of energy throughout the body, which runs along certain channels known as meridians. It is also believed that this energy exists throughout the universe and that all living creatures are dependent upon it as much as on physical nourishment. The energy is known by three similar names, *ki*, *chi* and *prana* in Japan, China and India respectively. (It should be noted that the term 'energy' in this context is not the same as the physical quantity that is measured in joules or calo-

ries.) As in acupuncture, there are certain pressure points
on the meridians that relate to certain organs, and these
points are known as *tsubos*.

Shiatsu can be used to treat a variety of minor problems
such as insomnia, headaches, anxiety, back pain, etc.
Western medicine may be unable to find a physical cause
for a problem, and although some pain relief may be pro-
vided, the underlying cause of the problem may not be
cured. It is possible that one session of shiatsu will be sufficient to remedy the problem by stimulating the flow of
energy along the channels. A regime of exercise (possibly
a specific routine) with a change in diet and/or lifestyle
may also be recommended. Shiatsu can encourage a general feeling of good health in the whole person, not just in
the physical sense. After some study or practice, shiatsu
can be performed on friends and relatives. There are many
benefits for both the giver and the receiver of shiatsu, both
on a physical and spiritual level.

Energy or ki

There are believed to be a number of auras, or energy layers, that surround the physical body and can be detected
or appreciated (figure 12). The first layer, the *etheric
body*, is the most dense and is connected with the body
and the way it works. An exercise is described later that
enables this layer to be detected. The *astral body* is much
wider, is affected by people's feelings and, if viewed by a
clairvoyant, is said to change in colour and shape depending on the feelings being experienced. The next aura is the
mental body, which is involved with the thought processes

figure 12: auras

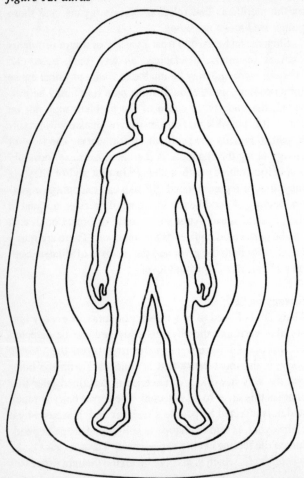

and intelligence of a person. Similarly, this can be viewed by a clairvoyant and is said to contain 'pictures' of ideas emanating from the person. These first three auras comprise the personality of a person. The last aura is known as the *causal body*, *soul* or *higher self*. This is concerned more with perceptive feelings and comprehension. It is believed in reincarnation that the first three auras die with the body, but the causal body carries on in its process of development by adopting another personality. As a person grows in maturity and awareness, these different auras are used, and energy is passed from one layer to another. It therefore follows that any alteration in the physical state will, in turn, affect the other layers, and vice versa.

Seven centres of energy, or chakras

It is believed that there are seven main *chakras* (a chakra being a centre of energy) found midway down the body, from the top of the head to the bottom of the torso. They are situated along the *sushumna*, or spiritual channel, which runs from the crown of the head to the base of the trunk. Energy enters the channel from both ends. Since the flow is most efficient when the back is straight, this is the ideal posture for meditation or when powers of concentration are required. Each chakra has a component of each aura, and it comprises what is known as a centre of consciousness. Each aura is activated as a person develops, and the same occurs with the chakras, beginning with the lowest (the *base chakra*) and progressing to the others with time. There is also a change of energy between the auras of each chakra (figure 13).

figure 2:
the Main
Chakras

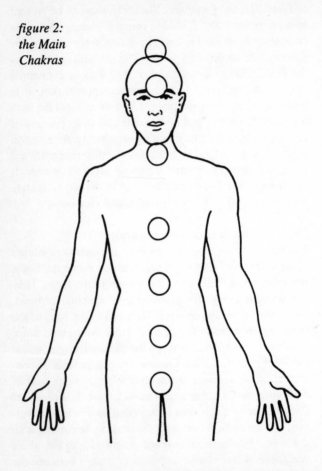

The *crown chakra* is concerned with the pineal gland, which controls the right eye and upper brain and affects spiritual matters. The *ajna* or *brow chakra* is linked with the pituitary gland, which controls the left eye, lower brain, nose and nervous system. It has an effect on the intellect, perception, intuition and comprehension. The *throat chakra* is concerned with the thyroid gland and governs the lymphatic system, hands, arms, shoulders, mouth, vocal cords, lungs and throat. It affects communication, creativity and self-expression. The *heart chakra* is concerned with the thymus gland and controls the heart, breasts, vagus nerve and circulatory system, and affects self-awareness, love, humanitarian acts and compassion. The *solar plexus chakra* is concerned with the pancreas. It controls the spleen, gall bladder, liver and digestive system and stomach, and has an effect on desire, personal power and the origin of emotions. The *sacral chakra* affects the gonads and controls the lower back, feet, legs and reproductive system. This affects physical, sexual and mental energy, relationships and self-worth. The *base chakra* is concerned with the adrenal glands. It controls the skeleton, parasympathetic and sympathetic nervous systems, bladder and kidneys, and affects reproduction and the physical will. As an example of this, if a person is suffering from an ailment of the throat, it is possible that he or she may also be unable to voice private thoughts and feelings.

Zang and fu organs

According to traditional Eastern therapies, organs have a

dual function—their physical one and another that is concerned with the use of energy and might be termed an 'energetic function'. The twelve organs mentioned in the traditional therapies are split into two groups known as *zang* and *fu*, and each is described below.

Zang organs are for energy storage, and the fu organs produce energy from sustenance and drink and also control excretion. The organs can be listed in pairs, each zang matched by a fu with a similar function. Although the pancreas is not specifically mentioned, it is usually included with the spleen. The same applies to the 'triple heater' or 'triple burner', which is connected with the solar plexus, lower abdomen and the thorax. The lungs are a zang organ and are concerned with assimilation of energy, or ki, from the air, which with energy from food ensures the complete body is fed and that mental alertness and a positive attitude are maintained. This is paired with the fu organ of the large intestine, which takes sustenance from the small intestine, absorbs necessary liquids and excretes waste material via the faeces. It is also concerned with self-confidence. The spleen is a zang organ and changes energy or ki from food into energy that is needed by the body. It is concerned with the mental functions of concentration, thinking and analysing. This is paired with the fu organ of the stomach, which prepares food so that nutrients can be extracted and also any energy, or ki, can be taken. It also provides 'food for thought'. The zang organ of the heart assists blood formation from ki and controls the flow of blood and the blood vessels. It is where the mind is housed and therefore affects awareness, belief,

long-term memory and feelings. This is paired with the fu
organ of the small intestine, which divides food into necessary and unnecessary parts, the latter passing to the
large intestine. It is also concerned with the making of de-
cisions. The kidneys are a zang organ and they produce
basic energy, or ki, for the other five paired organs and
also for reproduction, birth, development and maturity.
They also sustain the skeleton and brain and provide will-
power and 'get up and go'. They are paired with the fu organ of the bladder, which stores waste fluids until they are
passed as urine and also gives strength or courage. The
zang organ of the 'heart governor' is concerned with the
flow of blood throughout the body. It is a protector and
help for the heart and has a bearing on relationships with
other people (although there is no organ known as the
'heart governor' it is connected with the heart and its
functions). This is paired with the 'triple heater' or
'burner', which passes ki around the body and allows an
emotional exchange with others. The liver is the sixth
zang organ, and it assists with a regular flow of ki to
achieve the most favourable physiological effects and
emotional calmness. Positive feelings, humour, planning
and creativity are also connected with it. The gall bladder
is the sixth fu organ, with which the liver is paired, and
this keeps bile from the liver and passes it to the intestines. It concerns decision-making and forward thinking.

The meridian system
The meridians, as previously mentioned, are a system of

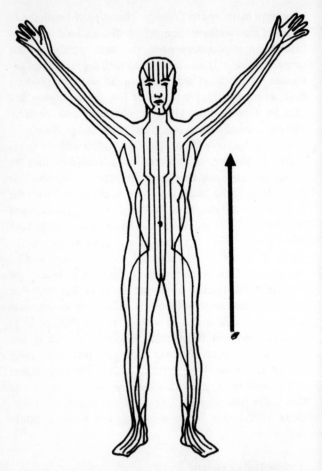

figure 14: the flow of energy along the meridians

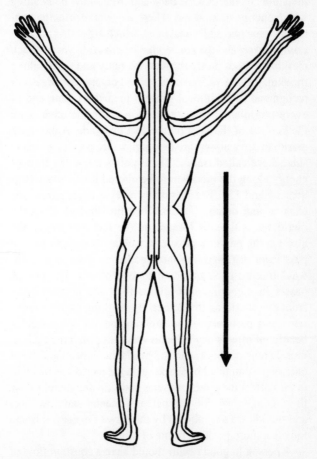

figure 15: the flow of energy along the meridians

invisible channels on the back and front of the body along which energy, or ki, flows. There are twelve principal meridians plus two additional ones, which are called *the governing vessel* and the *conception* or *directing vessel*. Each meridian passes partly through the body and partly along the skin, joining various chakras and organs (the organs as recognized in traditional Eastern medicine). One end of every meridian is beneath the skin while the other is on the surface of the skin on the feet or hands. Along each meridian are acupressure or acupuncture points, which in shiatsu are called *tsubos*. These points allow the flow of energy along the meridian to be altered if necessary (figures 14 and 15). The meridians receive energy from the chakras and organs (as described previously), from the meridians with ends located on the feet and hands and also via the pressure points, or tsubos. Energy, or ki, can pass from one meridian into another as there is a 'pathway' linking each meridian to two others. The energy passes in a continuous cycle or flow and in a set order from one meridian to another. By working on the meridians, and particularly the pressure points, a number of beneficial effects can be achieved with problems such as muscle tension, backache and headache. Since the flow of energy is stimulated by working on the meridians this will in turn affect the joints, muscles and skin and thereby ease these complaints. Since a person's mental state, feelings and moods are also altered by the flow of energy, this can induce a more positive frame of mind.

A person in good health should have a constant flow of ki, with no concentrations or imbalances in any part of the body. It is believed that the greater the amount of ki there is within a person's body, the greater the vitality, mental alertness and overall awareness that person will possess.

Feeling ki

It is possible for a person to 'feel' ki, and the following exercise helps demonstrate what it is like. Stand upright with the feet apart and the arms stretched upwards. Rub the hands together as if they were very cold, so that a feeling of warmth is generated. The backs of the hands, wrists and forearms should also be rubbed. The arms should be put down at the side of the body and shaken vigorously. This should then be repeated from the beginning, with the arms above the head and concluding with the shaking. Then hold the hands out to the front—they should have a pleasant feeling of warmth and vitality, which is due to the circulation of blood and energy that has been generated. The hands should be placed to the sides, then after inhaling deeply concentrate on relaxing as you exhale. This procedure should be done several times, and then it should be possible to feel the ki. The hands should be placed about 1 metre (3 feet) apart, with the palms of the hands facing inwards. After relaxation, concentrate your thoughts on the gap between your hands and then gradually reduce the space between them—but they must not touch. It is likely that when the hands come quite close, about 15–30 centimetres (6–12 inches), a feeling of tingling or warmth may be felt, or the sensation that there is something between the hands. This will be when the auras

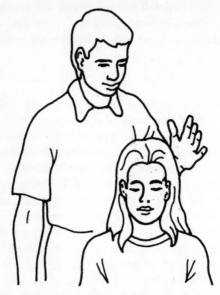

figure 16: feeling ki

that surround the hands touch. To reinforce the sensation, the hands should be taken apart again and then closed together so that the feeling is experienced again and becomes more familiar.

The following exercise also enables ki to be felt, but this time it is the etheric aura around another person's head and shoulders. The previous procedure to generate ki should be repeated, but this time the hand should be placed near to another person's head, within 60 centimetres–1 metre (2–3 feet). This person should be sitting up-

right on the floor or on a chair. The hand should be moved
gradually nearer to the seated person's head, concentrating attention on the gap between your hand and his or her
head. If no sensation is felt, the hand should be moved
back to its original position and the process should be repeated. Again, a feeling of tingling or warmth will probably be experienced as the person's aura is felt. When this
has been achieved, the hand can progress round the head
and down to the shoulders, noting the edge of the aura at
the same time (figure 16). If the person has no success in
experiencing the aura, it is likely that the mind is not clear
of other thoughts, so relaxation is suggested prior to any
further attempt.

It is also possible for a person, by concentrating his or
her thoughts and by a slight change of position, to alter the
flow of ki in the body. This will have the effect of either
making him or her feel a lot heavier or lighter, depending
on which is desired. Taken to extremes, someone who is
skilled at the control of ki will prove too heavy to be lifted
by four people.

Basic rules
There are some basic rules that should be followed before
the practice of shiatsu. Clothing should be comfortable,
loose-fitting and made of natural fibres since this will
help with the flow of energy or ki. The room should be
warm, quiet, have adequate space and be neat and clean. If
not, this can have an adverse effect on the flow of ki. The
person receiving the therapy should ideally lie on a futon
(a quilted Japanese mattress) or similar mat on the floor. If

necessary, pillows or cushions should be ready to hand if the person does not feel comfortable. Shiatsu should not be given or received by someone who has just eaten a large meal—it is advisable to delay for several hours. No pressure should be exerted on varicose veins or injuries such as cuts or breaks in bones. Although shiatsu can be of benefit to women while pregnant, there are four areas that should be avoided and these are the stomach, any part of the legs from the knees downwards, the fleshy web of skin between the forefinger and thumb, and an area on the shoulders at each side of the neck. Ensure that the person is calm and relaxed. It is generally not advisable to practise shiatsu on people who have serious illnesses such as heart disorders, multiple sclerosis or cancer. An experienced practitioner may be able to help, but a detailed and accurate diagnosis and course of treatment is essential. A verbal check on the person's overall health is important and also to ascertain if a woman is pregnant. If there is any worry or doubt about proceeding, then the safest option is not to go ahead.

Although the general feeling after receiving shiatsu is one of wellbeing and relaxation, there are occasionally unpleasant results, such as coughing, generation of mucus or symptoms of a cold; a feeling of tiredness; a headache or other pains and aches; or feeling emotional. The coughing and production of mucus is due to the body being encouraged to rid itself of its surplus foods (such as sugars and fats) in this form. A cold can sometimes develop when the mucus is produced, usually when the cells of the body are not healthy. Tiredness can occur, frequently with

a person who suffers from nervous tension. After therapy
has removed this stress or tension, then the body's need
for sleep and rest becomes apparent. A short-lived headache or other pain may also develop, for which there are
two main reasons. Since shiatsu redresses the balance of
ki in the body, this means that blockages in the flow of
energy are released and the ki can rush around the body,
causing a temporary imbalance in one part and resulting
in an ache or pain. It is also possible that too much time or
pressure may have been applied to a particular area. The
amount needed varies considerably from one person to
another. If a pain or headache is still present after a few
days, however, it is sensible to obtain qualified medical
help. Emotional feelings can occur while the energy is being stimulated to flow and balance is regained. The feelings may be connected with something from the past that
has been suppressed and so, when these emotions resur-
face, it is best for them to be expressed in a way that is
beneficial, such as crying. There may, of course, be no reaction at all. Some people are completely 'out of touch'
with their bodies and are aware only that all is not well
when pain is felt. If this is so, then any beneficial effects
from shiatsu may not register. Because of a modern diet
that contains an abundance of animal fats, people become
overweight through the deposition of fat below the skin
and around the internal organs. The body is unable to
'burn off' this fat, and this layer forms a barrier to ki. The
flow is stopped, and overweight people do not tend to
benefit as much because of the difficulty in stimulating
the flow of ki in the body.

figure 17: seiza

Exercises and the three main centres
The body is divided into three main centres—the *head*,
the *heart*, and the *abdominal* centres. The head centre is
concerned with activities of a mental nature, such as imaginative and intellectual thought processes, and is concerned with the brow chakra. The heart centre is concerned with interactions among people and to the world in
general, including the natural world. It is related to the
chakra of the throat and heart. The abdominal centre is related to the base, sacral and solar plexus chakras and is
concerned with the practical aspects of life and physical
activity. Ideally, energy should be divided equally among
the three but because of a number of factors, such as activ-

figure 18: inhaling via the nose

ity, education, diet, culture, etc, this is frequently not so. In shiatsu, more importance is attached to the abdominal centre, known as the *hara*. The following exercise uses abdominal breathing and, by so doing, not only is oxygen inhaled but also ki is taken into the hara where it increases a person's vitality. Once the technique is mastered, it can be practised virtually anywhere and will restore composure and calmness.

Sit on the floor with the back straight and, if possible, in the position known in Japan as *seiza* (figure 17). The hands should be placed loosely together in the lap and the mind and body should become relaxed after some deep breathing. One hand should be put on the stomach, below the navel, and the other on the chest. When inhaling, this should not be done with the chest but with the abdomen, which should increase in size. As the person exhales the abdomen should contract, and this procedure should be practised for a few minutes. After a rest it should be repeated, inhaling quite deeply but still the chest should not be allowed to rise. Some people may not find this exercise at all difficult while others may need more practice. It may be that there is stress or tension in the diaphragm. Once the technique has been mastered and the hands do not need to be placed on the chest and abdomen, imagine that ki is being inhaled down into the hara. Sit in the same position and inhale slowly via the nose and imagine the ki descending (figure 18). (It may aid concentration if the eyes are closed.) The breath should be held for about four seconds and concentration should be centred on the ki. Then exhale gradually through the mouth and repeat the process for a few minutes.

The next exercise is known as a centred movement.

figure 19

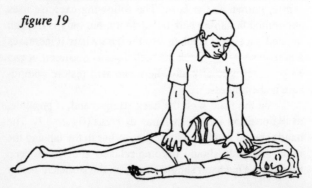

which practises movement of the ki, since it is one person's ki that should have an effect on another. After practising shiatsu on a partner, you should not feel tired but refreshed and exhilarated. This is a benefit of the extra ki in the body. The exercise should be begun on hands and knees (a body width apart), and it is most important that you are relaxed and comfortable with no tension. This position is the basis for other movements that are practised on others. While the position is maintained, begin to move the body backwards and forwards so that you are conscious of the transfer of weight, either on to the hands or knees. The body should then be moved slowly in a circular way, again being aware of the shift of weight from the hands, to hands and knees, to knees, etc, returning to the original position. You should also realize that as the whole body is moved, the abdomen is its 'centre of gravity'. Practise maintaining a position for about five seconds, registering the increase in weight on the hands when you move forwards and the reduction when you rock backwards. Then return to the original position. It is important that the body weight is always used at right angles to the receiver as this will have the maximum effect on the flow of ki. The reason for holding a particular position is that this has the effect of making the person's ki move.

The centred movement previously described can be practised on a partner in exactly the same way, following the same rules. The right hand should be placed on the sacrum, which is between the hips, and the left hand midway between the shoulder blades. As before, you should rock forwards and hold the position for about five seconds and then repeat after rocking backwards on to the knees (figure 19). This basic procedure can be repeated about twelve times, and if you are not sure whether too much or too little pressure is being used, check with your partner. You will eventually acquire the skill of knowing what amount is right for a particular person.

To summarize, there are some basic rules to be followed when practising shiatsu. A person should make use of body weight and not muscular strength, and there should be no effort involved. At all times a calm and relaxed state should be maintained, and the weight of the body should be at right angles in relation to the receiver's body. The person's whole body should be moved when altering weight on to the receiver, maintaining the hara as the centre. Any weight or pressure held should be for a short time only and both hands should be used equally. It is best to maintain a regular pattern of movement while giving shiatsu, and always keep in physical contact with the receiver by keeping a hand on him or her throughout the therapy.

There are a large number of different exercises and techniques, but at each time the giver must be relaxed and calm to enable the flow of ki to occur and thus make the shiatsu work to full effect. As an example, the following exercise on the face and head begins with the receiver's head being held firmly in one hand and, using the thumb of the other hand, pressing upwards in a straight line between the eyebrows towards the hairline. Each movement should only be quite small, about 12 millimetres (0.5 inch) (figure 20). The fingers

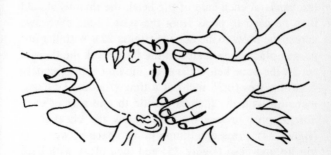

figure 20

figure 21

should then be placed on each side of the head and both
thumbs used to press from the inner end of the eyebrows towards the hairline (figure 21). Again, holding
the hands at each side of the head, the thumbs should
then be used to press from the start of the eyebrows
across the brow to the outside (figure 22). With the fingers in place at each side of the face, work the thumbs
across the bone below the eyes, moving approximately
6 millimetres (0.25 inch) at a time (figure 23). Com-
mencing with the thumbs a little to one side of each
nostril, press across the face below the cheekbones
(figure 24). Press one thumb in the space between the
top lip and nose (figure 25) and then press with both
the thumbs outwards over the upper jaw (figure 26).
Next, press one thumb in the hollow below the lower
lip and then press outwards with both thumbs over the
lower part of the jaw (figure 27). The giver then puts all
fingers of the hands beneath the lower jaw and then
leans backwards so that pressure is exerted (figure 28).

figure 22

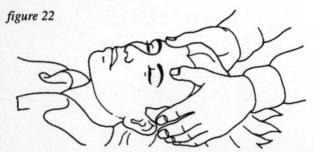

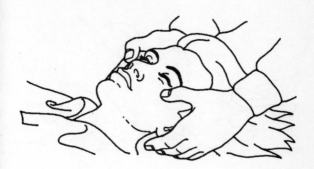

figure 23

figure 24

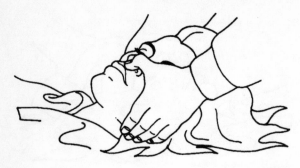

figure 25

figure 26

figure 27

figure 28

Kyo and jitsu energy

As a person progresses in the study of shiatsu and comes to understand the needs and requirements of others, he or she will gradually be able to give beneficial therapy. It is believed that energy, as previously defined, is the basis for all life, and it is divided into two types known as *kyo* and *jitsu*. If the energy is low or deficient, it is known as kyo, and if there is an excess or the energy is high, it is known as jitsu. These two factors will therefore affect the type of shiatsu that is given and, with practice, it should be possible to assess visually and also by touch what type a person is. A few general guidelines as to how a person can vary his or her shiatsu to suit either kyo or jitsu types are given below. As the person progresses, however, it is likely that an intuitive awareness will develop of what is most suitable for a particular person. For kyo types (low or deficient in energy), a gentle and sensitive touch is required, and any stretched positions can be maintained for a longer time as this will bring more energy to that part of the body. Pressure, held by the thumb or palm, can also be maintained for an increased length of time, approximately 10–15 seconds. For jitsu types (high or excess energy), the stretches can be done quite quickly so that the energy is dispersed, and also shaking or rocking areas of the body can have the same effect. The pressure that is exerted by the thumbs or palms should also be held for a shorter length of time, so that excess energy is dispelled.

Yin and yang

As previously mentioned, a change in diet may also be

recommended by a shiatsu practitioner. From the view-point of traditional Oriental medicine, food can be defined in an 'energetic' way. This differs from the Western defi-nition of foods consisting of protein, minerals, fats, carbo-hydrates, fibre and vitamins. It is believed that, according to its 'energetic' definition, food will have differing physical, mental, spiritual and emotional effects. This en-ergy is split into two parts known as *yin* and *yang*. Yin is where energy is expanding and yang where it is contract-ing. They are thus opposites and, from traditional beliefs, it was thought that interactions between them formed all manner of occurrences in nature and the whole of the world and beyond. All definitions of yin and yang are based on macrobiotic food (a diet intended to prolong life, comprised of pure vegetable foods such as brown rice), this being the most usual reference. Food can be divided into three main types—those that are 'balanced', and some that are yin and some that are yang. Foods that are defined as being yin are milk, alcohol, honey, sugar, oil, fruit juices, spices, stimulants, most drugs (such as aspi-rin, etc), tropical vegetables and fruits, refined foods, and most food additives of a chemical nature. Yang foods are poultry, seafood, eggs, meat, salt, fish, miso and cheese. Balanced foods are seeds, nuts, vegetables, cereal grains, beans, sea vegetables and temperate fruits (such as apples and pears).

The balance between yin and yang is very important to the body, for example, in the production of hormones such as oestrogen and progesterone, and glycogen and insulin and the expansion and contraction of the lungs, etc. A 'balanced' way of eating, mainly from the grains, beans, seeds, nuts and vegetables, etc, is important as this will help to achieve the energy balance in the meridians, organs and chakras, as defined previously. When these two opposing forces of yin and yang are in harmony and balanced, physical and mental health will result.

Body reading

It is possible for practitioners of shiatsu, as they become increasingly experienced, to assess a person's physical and mental state of health by observing the body and forming accurate observations. If the traditional ways of Eastern diagnosis are studied, this can assist greatly. The Eastern methods were based on the senses of hearing, seeing, smelling and touching and also by questioning people to obtain information leading to an overall diagnosis. This is known as body reading.

Makko-ho exercises

Makko-ho exercises are six stretching exercises, each of which affects one pair of the meridians by stimulating its flow of energy. If the complete set of exercises is performed, all the body's meridians will have been stimulated in turn, which should result in increased vigour and an absence of tiredness. Before beginning the exercises, you should feel calm and relaxed. It may prove beneficial to perform some abdominal breathing first (as previously described). One example is the triple heater and heart governor meridian stretch. Sit on the ground with either the feet together or crossed. The right hand should grasp the left knee and the left hand the right knee, both quite

figure 29

figure 30

firmly (figure 29). Then inhale and, as you exhale, lean forwards and downwards with the top half of the body so that the knees are pushed apart (figure 30). Hold this position for approximately 30 seconds while breathing normally, and then, after inhaling, return to the upright position. After completion of all exercises, lie flat on the ground for several minutes and relax.

Acupressure

This is an ancient form of healing combining massage and acupuncture, practised over 3,000 years ago in Japan and China. It was developed into its current form using a system of special massage points and is today still practised widely in the Japanese home environment.

Certain 'pressure points' are located in various parts of the body, and these are used by the practitioner by massaging firmly with the thumb or fingertip. These points are the same as those utilized in acupuncture. There are various ways of working, and the pressure can be applied by the practitioner's fingers, thumbs, knees, palms of the hand, etc. Relief from pain can be quite rapid at times, depending upon its cause, while other more persistent problems can take longer to improve.

Acupressure is said to enhance the body's own method of healing, thereby preventing illness and improving the energy level. The pressure exerted is believed to regulate a matter called *qi*, which is energy that flows along 'meridians'. These are invisible channels that run along the length of the body. These meridians are mainly named after the organs of the body, such as the liver and stomach, but there are four exceptions, which are called the 'pericardium', 'triple heater', 'conception' and 'governor'. Specifically named meridian lines may also be used to treat ailments other than those relating to it.

Ailments claimed to have been treated successfully are back pain, asthma, digestive problems, insomnia, migraine and circulatory problems, amongst others. Changes in diet, regular exercise and certain self-checking methods may be recommended by your practitioner. It must be borne in mind that some painful symptoms are the onset of serious illness so you should always first consult your GP.

Before any treatment begins, a patient will be asked details of lifestyle and diet. The pulse rate will be taken, along with any relevant past history relating to the current problem. The person will be requested to lie on a mattress on the floor or on a firm table, and comfortable but loose-fitting clothing is best so that the practitioner can work most effectively on the energy channels. No oils are used on the body, and there is no equipment. Each session lasts from approximately 30 minutes to 1 hour. Once the pressure is applied, and this can be done in a variety of ways particular to each practitioner, varying sensations may be felt. Some points may feel sore or tender, and there may be some discomfort such as a deep pain or coolness. It is believed, however, that this form of massage works quickly so that any tenderness soon passes.

The number of treatments will vary from patient to patient, according to how the person responds and what problem or ailment is being treated. Weekly visits may be needed if a specific disorder is being treated while other people may go whenever they feel in need. It is advisable for women who are pregnant to check with their practitioner first since some of the acupressure methods are not

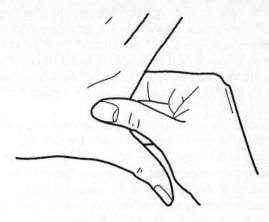

figure 31: large intestine 4

recommended during pregnancy. Acupressure can be
practised safely at home although it is usually better for
one person to perform the massage on another. Common
problems such as headache, constipation and toothache
can be treated quite simply, although there is the possibility of any problem worsening first before an improvement
occurs if the pressure points are over-stimulated. You
should, however, see your doctor if any ailment persists.
To treat headache, facial soreness, toothache and men-
strual pain, locate the fleshy piece of skin between the
thumb and forefinger and squeeze firmly, pressing towards the forefinger. The pressure should be applied for
about five minutes and either hand can be used. This point
is known as *large intestine 4* (figure 31).

To aid digestive problems in both adults and babies, for

example to settle infantile colic, the point known as *stomach 36* is utilized, which is located on the outer side of the leg about 75 millimetres (3 inches) down from the knee. This point should be quite simple to find as it can often feel slightly tender. It should be pressed quite firmly and strongly for about five to ten minutes with the thumb (figure 32).

When practising acupressure massage on someone else and before treatment begins, ensure that the person is warm, relaxed, comfortable and wearing loose-fitting clothing and that he or she is lying on a firm mattress or rug on the floor. To discover the areas that need to be worked on, press firmly over the body and see which areas are tender. These tender areas on the body correspond to an organ that is not working correctly. To begin massage using fingertips or thumbs, a pressure of about 4.5 kilograms (10 pounds) should be exerted. The massage movements should be performed very quickly, about 50 to 100 times every minute, and some discomfort is likely

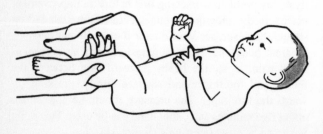

figure 32: utilizing stomach 36

(which will soon pass) but there should be no pain. Particular care should be taken to avoid causing pain on the face, stomach or over any joints. If a baby or young child is being massaged then considerably less pressure should be used. If there is any doubt as to the correct amount, exert a downwards pressure on bathroom scales to ascertain the weight being used. There is no need to hurry from one point to another since approximately 5 to 15 minutes is needed at each for adults, but only about 30 seconds for babies or young children.

Using 'self-help' acupressure, massage can be repeated as often as is felt to be necessary with several sessions per hour usually being sufficient for painful conditions that have arisen suddenly. It is possible that as many as 20 sessions may be necessary for persistent conditions causing pain, with greater intervals of time between treatments as matters improve. It is not advisable to try anything that is at all complicated (or to treat an illness such as arthritis), and a trained practitioner will obviously be able to provide the best level of treatment and help. To contact a reputable practitioner who has completed the relevant training it is advisable to contact the appropriate professional body.

Acupuncture

This is an ancient Chinese therapy that involves inserting needles into the skin at specific points of the body. The word 'acupuncture' originated from a Dutch physician, William Ten Rhyne, who had been living in Japan during the latter part of the 17th century, and it was he who introduced it to Europe. The term means literally 'prick with a needle'. The earliest textbook on acupuncture, dating from approximately 400 BC, was called *Nei Ching Su Wen*, which means 'Yellow Emperor's Classic of Internal Medicine'. Also recorded at about the same time was the successful saving of a patient's life by acupuncture, the person having been expected to die while in a coma. Legend has it that acupuncture was developed when it was realized that soldiers who recovered from arrow wounds were sometimes also healed of other diseases from which they were suffering. Acupuncture was very popular with British doctors in the early 1800s for pain relief and to treat fever. There was also a specific article on the successful treatment of rheumatism that appeared in *The Lancet*. Until the end of the Ching dynasty in China in 1911, acupuncture was slowly developed and improved, but then medicine from the West increased in popularity. More recently, however, there has been a revival of interest, and it is again widely practised throughout China.

Also, nowadays the use of laser beams and electrical currents are found to give an increased stimulative effect when using acupuncture needles.

The specific points of the body into which acupuncture needles are inserted are located along 'meridians'. These are the pathways or energy channels and are believed to be related to the internal organs of the body. This energy is known as *qi*, and the needles are used to decrease or increase the flow of energy or to unblock it if it is impeded. Traditional Chinese medicine sees the body as being comprised of two natural forces, known as the *yin* and *yang* *(figure 33)*. These two forces are complementary to each other but also opposing, the yin being the female force—calm and passive and also representing the dark, cold,

figure 33: yin and yang

swelling and moisture. The yang force is the male and is stimulating and aggressive, representing heat and light, contraction and dryness. It is believed that the cause of ailments and diseases is due to an imbalance of these forces in the body, for example, if a person is suffering from a headache or high blood pressure then this is because of an excess of yang. If, however, there is an excess of yin, this might result in tiredness, feeling cold and fluid retention (figure 33)

The aim of acupuncture is to establish that there is an imbalance of yin and yang and to rectify it by using the needles at certain points on the body. Traditionally there were 365 points but more have been found in the intervening period, and nowadays there can be as many as 2,000. There are 14 meridians, 12 of which are illustrated in figure 34, called after the organs they represent, for example, the lung, kidney, heart and stomach as well as two organs unknown in orthodox medicine—the triple heater or warmer, which relates to the activity of the endocrine glands and the control of temperature. In addition, the pericardium is concerned with seasonal activity and also regulates the circulation of the blood. Of the 14 meridians, there are two, known as the 'du' or 'governor' and the 'ren' or 'conception', which both run straight up the body's midline, although the du is much shorter, extending from the head down to the mouth, while the ren starts at the chin and extends to the base of the trunk.

There are several factors that can change the flow of qi (also known as shi or ch'i), and they can be of an emotional, physical or environmental nature. The flow may be changed to become too slow or fast, it can be diverted or

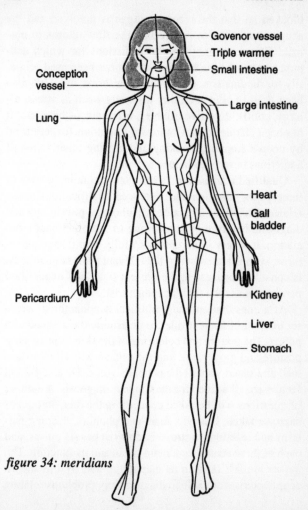

Govenor vessel
Triple warmer
Small intestine
Conception vessel
Lung
Large intestine
Heart
Gall bladder
Pericardium
Kidney
Liver
Stomach

figure 34: meridians

blocked so that the incorrect organ is involved and the acupuncturist has to ensure that the flow returns to normal. There are many painful afflictions for which acupuncture can be used. In the West, it has been used primarily for rheumatism, back pain and arthritis, but it has also been used to alleviate other disorders, such as stress, allergy, colitis, digestive troubles, insomnia, asthma, etc. It has been claimed that withdrawal symptoms (experienced by people stopping smoking and ceasing other forms of addiction) have been helped as well.

Qualified acupuncturists complete a training course of three years' duration and also need qualifications in the related disciplines of anatomy, pathology, physiology and diagnosis before they can belong to a professional association. It is very important that a fully qualified acupuncturist, who is a member of the relevant professional body, is consulted because at the present time, any unqualified person can use the title 'acupuncturist'.

At a consultation, the traditional acupuncturist uses a set method of ancient rules to determine the acupuncture points. The texture and colouring of the skin, type of skin, posture and movement, and the tongue will all be examined and noted, as will the patient's voice. These different factors are all needed for the Chinese diagnosis. A number of questions will be asked concerning the diet, amount of exercise taken, lifestyle, fears and phobias, sleeping patterns and reactions to stress. Each wrist has six pulses, and each of these stands for a main organ and its function. The pulses are felt (known as palpating), and by this means acupuncturists are able to diagnose any problems relating to the flow of qi and if there is any disease present in the internal organs. The first consultation may last an hour, especially if detailed questioning is necessary along with the palpation.

The needles used in acupuncture are disposable and made of a fine stainless steel and come already sealed in a sterile pack. They can be sterilized by the acupuncturist in a machine known as an autoclave but using boiling water is not adequate for this purpose. (Diseases such as HIV and hepatitis can be passed on by using unsterilized needles.) Once the needle is inserted into the skin, it is twisted between the acupuncturist's thumb and forefinger to spread or draw the energy from a point. The depth to which the needle is inserted can vary from just below the skin to up to 12 millimetres (half an inch), and different sensations may be felt, such as a tingling around the area of insertion or a loss of sensation at that point. Up to 15 needles can be used but around five is generally sufficient. The length of time that they are left in varies from a few minutes to half an hour, and this is dependent on a number of factors, such as how the patient has reacted to previous treatment and the ailment from which he or she is suffering.

Patients can generally expect to feel an improvement after four to six sessions of therapy, the beneficial effects occurring gradually, particularly if the ailment has obvious and long-standing symptoms. Other diseases such as asthma will probably take longer before any definite improvement is felt. It is possible that some patients may not feel any improvement at all, or even feel worse after the first session, and this is probably due to the energies in the body being over-stimulated. To correct this, the acupuncturist will gradually use fewer needles and for a shorter period of time. If no improvement is felt after about six to eight treatments, then it is doubtful whether acupuncture will be of any help. For general body maintenance and health, most traditional acupuncturists suggest that sessions be arranged at the time of seasonal changes.

There has been a great deal of research, particularly by the Chinese, who have produced many books detailing a high success rate for acupuncture in treating a variety of disorders. These results are, however, viewed cautiously in the West as methods of conducting clinical trials vary from East to West. Nevertheless, trials have been carried out in the West, and it has been discovered that a pain message can be stopped from reaching the brain using acupuncture. The signal would normally travel along a nerve but it is possible to 'close a gate' on the nerve, thereby preventing the message from reaching the brain, hence preventing the perception of pain. Acupuncture is believed to work by blocking the pain signal. Doctors stress, however, that pain can be a warning of something wrong or of a particular disease such as cancer, which requires an orthodox remedy or method of treatment.

It has also been discovered that there are substances produced by the body that are connected with pain relief. These substances are called endorphins and encephalins, and they are natural opiates. Studies from all over the world show that acupuncture stimulates the release of these opiates into the central nervous system, thereby giving pain relief. The amount of opiates released has a direct

bearing on the degree of pain relief. Acupuncture is a
widely used form of anaesthesia in China where, for suitable patients, it is said to be extremely effective (90 per
cent). It is used successfully during childbirth, dentistry
and for operations. Orthodox doctors in the West now accept that heat treatment, massage and needles used on a
sensitive part of the skin afford relief from pain caused by
disease elsewhere. These areas are known as trigger
points, and they are not always situated close to the organ
that is affected by disease. It has been found that approximately three-quarters of these trigger points are the same
as the points used in Chinese acupuncture. Recent research has also shown that it is possible to find the acupuncture points by the use of electronic instruments, as
they register less electrical resistance than other areas of
skin. As yet, no evidence has been found to substantiate
the existence of meridians.

The Alexander Technique

This technique, which is based on correct posture so that the body is able to function naturally and with the minimum amount of muscular effort, was devised by Frederick Mathias Alexander (1869–1955). He was an Australian actor who found that he was losing his voice when performing, but after rest his condition improved. Although he received medical help, the condition did not improve, and it occurred to him that while acting he might be doing something that caused the problem. To see what this might be, he performed his act in front of a mirror and saw what happened when he was about to speak. He experienced difficulty in breathing and lowered his head, thus making himself shorter. He realized that the strain of remembering his lines and having to project his voice, so that the people farthest away in the audience would be able to hear him, was causing him a great deal of stress, and the way he reacted was a quite natural reflex action. In fact, even thinking about having to project his voice made the symptoms recur, and from this he concluded that there must be a close connection between body and mind. He was determined to try to improve the situation, and gradually, by watching and altering his stance and posture and his mental attitude to his performance on stage, matters improved. He was able to act and speak on stage and use his body in a more relaxed and natural fashion.

In 1904 Alexander travelled to London where he had decided to let others know about his method of retraining the body. He soon became very popular with other actors who appreciated the benefits of using his technique. Other public figures, such as the author Aldous Huxley, also benefited. Later he went to America, achieving considerable success and international recognition for his technique. At the age of 78 he suffered a stroke, but by using his method he managed to regain the use of all his faculties—an achievement that amazed his doctors.

The Alexander technique is said to be completely harmless, encouraging an agreeable state between mind and body and is also helpful for a number of disorders such as headaches and back pain. Today, Alexander training schools can be found all over the world. A simple test to determine if people can benefit is to observe their posture. People frequently do not even stand correctly, and this can encourage aches and pains if the body is unbalanced. It is incorrect to stand with round shoulders or to slouch. This often looks uncomfortable, and discomfort may be felt. Sometimes people will hold themselves too erect and unbending, which again can have a bad effect. The correct posture and balance for the body needs the least muscular effort but the body will be aligned correctly (figures 35, 36 and 37). When walking one should not slouch, hold the head down or have the shoulders stooped. The head should be balanced correctly above the spine with the shoulders relaxed. It is suggested that the weight of the body should be felt being transferred from one foot to the other while walking.

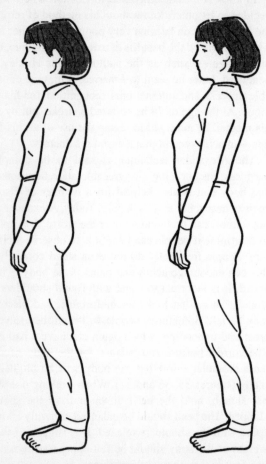

figures 35, 36 and 37: posture

Once a teacher has been consulted, all movements and how the body is used will be observed. Many muscles are used in everyday activities, and over the years bad habits can develop unconsciously, with stress also affecting the use of muscles. This can be demonstrated in people gripping a pen with too much force or holding the steering wheel of a car too tightly when driving. Muscular tension can be a serious problem affecting some people, and the head, neck and back are forced out of line, which, in turn, leads to rounded shoulders, with the head held forward and the back curved. If this situation is not altered, and the body is not realigned correctly, the spine will become curved with a hump possibly developing. This leads to back pain and puts a strain on internal organs such as the chest and lungs.

No force is used by the teacher other than some gentle manipulation to start pupils off correctly. Some teachers use light pushing methods on the back and hips, etc, while others might first ensure that the pupil is relaxed and then pull gently on the neck, which stretches the body. Any bad postures will be corrected by the teacher, and the pupil will

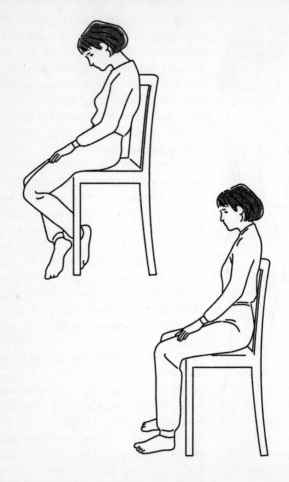

figures 38 and 39: posture when seated

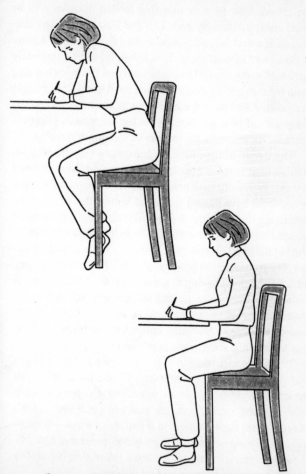

figures 40 and 41: posture when seated at a table

be shown how best to alter this so that muscles will be used most effectively and with the least effort. Any manipulation that is used will be to ease the body into a more relaxed and natural position. It is helpful to be completely aware of using the technique not only on the body but also with the mind. With frequent use of the Alexander technique for posture and the release of tension, the muscles and the body should be used correctly with a consequent improvement in, for example, the manner of walking and sitting.

The length of time for each lesson can vary from about half an hour to three quarters of an hour and the number of lessons is usually between 10 and 30, by which time pupils should have gained sufficient knowledge to continue practising the technique by themselves. Once a person has learned how to improve posture, it will be found that he or she is taller and carrying the body in a more upright manner. The technique has been found to be of benefit to dancers, athletes and those having to speak in public. Other disorders claimed to have been treated successfully are depressive states, headaches caused by tension, anxiety, asthma, hypertension, respiratory problems, colitis, osteoarthritis and rheumatoid arthritis, sciatica and peptic ulcer.

The Alexander technique is recommended for all ages and types of people, as their overall quality of life, both mental and physical, can be improved. People can learn how to resist stress, and one eminent professor experienced a great improvement in a variety of ways—in quality of sleep, lessening of high blood pressure, and improved mental awareness. He even found that his ability to play a musical instrument had improved.

The Alexander technique can applied to two positions adopted every day, namely sitting in a chair and sitting at a desk. To be seated in the correct manner the head should be comfortably balanced, with no tension in the shoulders, and a small gap between the knees (if legs are crossed the spine and pelvis become out of line or twisted) and the soles of the feet should be flat on the floor. It is incorrect to sit with the head lowered and the shoulders slumped forward because the stomach becomes restricted and breathing may also be affected. On the other hand, it is also incorrect to hold the body in a stiff and erect position (*see* figures 38 and 39 on page 110).

To sit correctly while working at a table, the body should be held upright but in a relaxed manner with any bending movement coming from the hips and with the seat flat on the chair. If writing, the pen should be held lightly, and if using a computer one should ensure that the arms are relaxed and feel comfortable. The chair should be set at a comfortable height with regard to the level of the desk. It is incorrect to lean forward over a desk because this hampers breathing, or to hold the arms in a tense, tight manner (*see* figures 40 and 41 on page 111).

There has been some scientific research carried out that concurs with the beliefs that Alexander formed, such as the relationship between mind and body (the thought of doing an action actually triggering a physical reaction or tension). Today, doctors do not have any opposition to the Alexander technique and may recommend it on occasions.

Chiropractic

The word chiropractic originates from two Greek words—*kheir*, which means 'hand', and *praktikos*, which means 'practical'. A school of chiropractic was established in about 1895 by a healer called Daniel Palmer (1845–1913). He was able to cure a man's deafness, which had occurred when he bent down and felt a bone click. Upon examination, Palmer discovered that some bones of the man's spine had become displaced. After successful manipulation the man regained his hearing. Palmer formed the opinion that if there was any displacement in the skeleton this could affect the function of nerves, either increasing or decreasing their action and thereby resulting in a malfunction, i.e. a disease.

Chiropractic is used to relieve pain by manipulation and to correct any problems that are present in joints and muscles but especially the spine. Like osteopathy, no use is made of surgery or drugs. If there are any spinal disorders they can cause widespread problems elsewhere in the body, such as the hip, leg or arm, and can also initiate lumbago, sciatica, a slipped disc or other back problems. It is even possible that spinal problems can result in seemingly unrelated problems such as catarrh, migraine, asthma, constipation, stress, etc. However, the majority of a chiropractor's patients suffer mainly from neck and back pain. People suffering from whiplash injuries sustained in car accidents commonly seek the help of a chiropractor (figure 42). The whiplash effect is caused when the head is violently wrenched either forwards or backwards at the time of impact.

Another common problem that chiropractors treat is headaches, and it is often the case that tension is the underlying cause, as it makes the neck muscles contract. Athletes can also obtain relief from injuries such as tennis

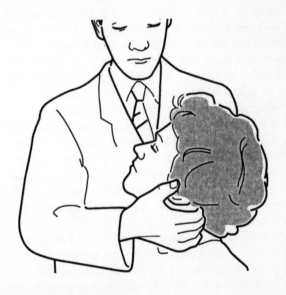

figure 42: manipulative treatment for a whiplash injury

elbow, pulled muscles, injured ligaments and sprains, etc. As well as the normal methods of manipulating joints, the chiropractor may decide it is necessary to use applications of ice or heat to relieve the injury.

Children can also benefit from treatment by the chiropractor, as there may be some slight accident that occurs in their early years that can reappear in adult life in the form of back pain. It can easily happen, for example, when a child learns to walk and bumps into furniture, or when a baby falls out of a cot. This could result in damage to the spine, which will show only in adult life when a person experiences back pain. At birth, a baby's neck may be injured or the spine may be strained if the use of forceps is necessary, and this can result in headaches and neck problems as he or she grows to maturity. This early type of injury could also account for what is known as 'growing pains', when the real problem is actually damage that has been done to the bones or muscles. If a parent has any worries it is best to consult a doctor, and it is possible that the child will be recommended to see a qualified chiropractor. To avoid any problems in adult life, chiropractors recommend that children have occasional examinations to detect any damage or displacement in bones and muscles.

As well as babies and children, adults of all ages can benefit from chiropractic. There are some people who regularly take painkillers for painful joints or back pain, but this does not deal with the root cause of the pain, only the symptoms that are produced. It is claimed that chiropractic could be of considerable help in giving treatment

to these people. Many pregnant women experience backache at some stage during their pregnancy because of the
extra weight that is placed on the spine, and they also may
find it difficult keeping their balance. At the time of giving birth, changes take place in the pelvis and joints at the
bottom of the spine, and this can be a cause of back pain.
Lifting and carrying babies, if not done correctly, can also
damage the spine and thereby make the back painful.

It is essential that any chiropractor is fully qualified
and registered with the relevant professional association.
At the initial visit, a patient will be asked for details of his
or her case history, including the present problem, and
during the examination painful and tender areas will be
noted and joints will be checked to see whether they are
functioning correctly or not. X-rays are frequently used
by chiropractors as these help them to make a detailed diagnosis since they can show signs of bone disease, fractures or arthritis as well as the spine's condition. After the
initial visit, any treatment will normally begin as soon as
the patient has been informed of the chiropractor's diagnosis. If it has been decided that chiropractic therapy will
not be of any benefit, the patient will be advised accordingly.

For treatment, underwear and/or a robe will be worn,
and the patient will either lie, sit or stand on a specially
designed couch. Chiropractors use their hands in a skilful
way to effect the different manipulative techniques. If it is
decided that manipulation is necessary to treat a painful
lumbar joint, the patient will need to lie on his or her side.
The upper and lower spine will then be rotated manually

but in opposite ways. This manipulation will have the effect of partially locking the joint that is being treated, and the upper leg is usually flexed to aid the procedure. The vertebra that is immediately below or above the joint will then be felt by the chiropractor, and the combination of how the patient is lying, coupled with gentle pressure applied by the chiropractor's hand, will move the joint to its farthest extent of normal movement. There will then be a very quick push applied on the vertebra, which results in its movement being extended farther than normal, ensuring that full use of the joint is regained. This is due to the muscles that surround the joint being suddenly stretched, which has the effect of relaxing the muscles of the spine that work upon the joint. This alteration should cause the joint to be able to be used more naturally and should not be a painful procedure.

There can be a variety of effects felt after treatment. Some patients may feel sore, stiff or may ache for some time after the treatment, while others will experience the lifting of pain at once. In some cases there may be a need for multiple treatments, perhaps four or more, before improvement is felt. On the whole, problems that have been troubling a patient for a considerable time (chronic) will need more therapy than anything that occurs quickly and is very painful (acute).

Although there are only quite a small number of chiropractors in the UK—yet this numbers is increasing—there is a degree of contact and liaison between them and doctors. It is generally accepted that chiropractic is an effective remedy for bone and muscular problems, and the majority of doctors would be happy to accept a chiropractor's diagnosis and treatment, although the treatment of any general diseases, such as diabetes or asthma, would not be viewed in the same manner.

Do-in

Do-in (pronounced doe-in) is another ancient type of massage that originated in China. It is a technique of self-massage and, as in other forms of alternative therapy, it is believed that there is a flow of energy throughout the body that travels along 'meridians', and that each one of these is connected to a vital organ, such as the lungs, liver and heart. Do-in has a connection with shiatsu, and people of any age can participate, the only stipulation being that they be active and not out of condition. Clothing should not be tight or restrictive and adequate space is needed to perform the exercises.

If do-in is to be used as an invigorating form of massage then the best time of day is as soon as possible after rising but not after breakfast. After meals are the only times when do-in is to be avoided. It is generally recommended that people wishing to practise do-in should first go to classes where it is being taught, so that when the exercises are done at home they are performed correctly. It is claimed that the use of do-in is preventive in nature since the vital organs are strengthened and therefore maintained in a healthy state. As in massage, this is a deterrent to the nervous tension, strain and stress experienced by many people in modern life. It is also claimed to be beneficial for people suffering from arthritis and rheumatism.

Before starting it is best to do some warming-up exercises so that the body is not stiff. Begin by sitting on the ground with the knees up, grasp the knees and begin a rocking motion forwards and backwards (figure 43). Then sit up, again on the floor, position the legs as if to sit cross-legged but put the soles of the feet touching each other. Hold the toes for a short time. These two exercises should help to make the body more supple.

For the spleen meridian exercise, which is connected with the stomach, stand as near as possible in front of a wall. Place one hand palm downwards high up the wall so that there is a good stretching action and with the other hand grasp the foot that is opposite to the raised arm. Then the neck and head should be stretched backwards, away

figure 43: a warming-up exercise

from the wall. Maintain this stretched position and inhale and exhale deeply twice and then relax. Repeat the procedure using the other arm and leg (figure 44).

For the bladder meridian exercise, and thereby the kidneys, sit on the floor with the legs straight out in front and ensure that the toes are tensed upright. The arms should then be stretched above the head and a breath taken. After breathing out, bend forwards from the shoulders with the arms in front and hold the toes. Maintain this for the length of time it takes to breathe in and out three times. Repeat the whole procedure again (figure 45).

To do the exercise for the pericardium meridian, which affects the circulation, sit on the floor with feet touching, but one behind the other, ensuring that the hands are crossed and touching opposite knees. Grasp the knees and in-

figure 44: the spleen meridian exercise

figure 45:
the bladder
meridian
exercise

cline the body forwards with the aim of pushing the knees downwards on to the floor. Do this exercise again but with the hands on opposite knees and the other foot on the outside.

Using the exercise that strengthens the large intestine

*figure 46: the large
intestine meridian
exercise*

meridian and in turn the lungs, stand upright with the feet apart. Link the thumbs behind the back and then inhale. Exhale and at the same time place the arms outwards and upwards behind the back. To complete the exercise, lean forwards from the hips and then stand upright (figure 46).

To strengthen the liver by stimulating the gall bladder meridian, sit upright on the floor with the legs the maximum distance apart. Then inhale, passing the arms along the length of the right leg so that the base of the foot can be held. There should be no movement of the buttocks off the floor. Maintain this stretched position while breathing deeply twice. Repeat the exercise using the other leg.

After all exercises have been accomplished, lie flat out on the floor with the legs apart and the arms stretched at the sides, palms uppermost. Then lift the head so that the feet can be seen and then put the head back on the floor again. The head and body should then be shaken so that the legs, arms and neck are loosened. To complete the relaxation, the eyes should be closed and the person should lie quietly for a few minutes.

Hypnotherapy

The word 'hypnotherapy' is based on the term 'hypnosis', which is derived from the Greek word *hypnos*, meaning 'sleep'. The word 'hypnosis' was invented in the 19th century by James Braid, a Scottish surgeon who sometimes used the technique of mesmerism while performing operations. He was not the only doctor to practise hypnotism at that time, and in India, James Esdaile used it as the sole anaesthetic for many operations. This was in complete contravention to medical opinion at that time, since for over 50 years the practice and theory of mesmerism had been condemned.

Mesmerism originated with Dr Franz Mesmer (1734–1815), who became convinced from his research into the power and use of magnets that magnetism existed as an unseen fluid that passed through and joined everything in the world. Magnets and powers of hypnosis seem to have been used for centuries, whether in ancient Greece, by medicine men and witch doctors, or by priests. Mesmer believed that illness was precipitated when this force did not flow freely and that to cure ailments the use of magnets was necessary to correct the flow. For a time his popularity increased in his practice in Vienna, but when unsuccessful cases occurred, he was criticized by the University and forced to leave the city. After moving to Paris in 1778 he again found fame by having a clientele who came for the theatrical atmosphere and effects as well as to be cured. His patients were put into a trance by the combination of soft lights and music as they stood holding onto a container that held iron filings and water. Dr Mesmer held that they then received the effects of the 'magnetism' while he held a rod made of iron. Nowadays, it is thought that his strong personality, charisma and powers of suggestion were the source of any cures, with his patients actually being 'mesmerized'. After investigation by the French medical profession and establishment, no scientific basis to his practice was found. They also did not approve of the methods he used and were aware of the scandal connected with his name. He was later known as a quack and his methods faded into obscurity.

With the advent of new anaesthetics such as chloroform and ether, the technique of hypnotherapy fell out of use, although it was obvious that it could successfully deaden pain. Around the 1900s, hypnotism was again investigated by the British Medical Association, but approval was not forthcoming. It has only recently regained some popularity, with hypnotherapists viewing the trance as a condition in which body and mind can be calm and serene. While in this state, alterations can be made that are not achievable while the patient is completely conscious. The state of being neither fully awake nor fully asleep can be compared to when a person is 'miles away', i.e. daydreaming, or to a person who is sleepwalking. While in a trance a person can function correctly and carry out tasks, converse sensibly and carry out requests. Unlike a sleepwalker, who is in charge of his or her own actions, a person in a trance is open to requests or suggestions from the therapist. The changes that can be effected can be either mental or physical, such as the lessening of pain, healing disorders and encouraging relaxation. Sometimes, a patient may have a problem that originates with an event that happened some time ago, for example, in their childhood. If this is the case, and the patient can be helped to accept what has happened in the past through the use of hypnotherapy, this can also boost morale and self-confidence.

The aim of hypnotherapy is that the patient and therapist work together to achieve a cure or overcome some difficulty. There are a variety of disorders that have been treated with success, such as migraine, irritable bowel syndrome, ulcers and skin disorders, along with other problems caused by stress and anxiety. Illnesses known as hysterical illness are a relatively common problem that hypnotherapists treat. They include phobias (a fear of flying, heights, etc), insomnia and asthma. The pain of childbirth can also be relieved.

To ensure that any hypnotherapist is fully trained, it is advisable to contact the relevant professional organization. As well as the hypnotherapist being fully trained, a patient must feel that he or she can trust and talk openly to his or her therapist on personal matters, if need be. The nature and character of the therapist is therefore also extremely important so that the two can work together to alleviate the problem. The cost of private sessions can vary considerably, and the number needed is also variable, although on average it is likely to be between five and ten, depending on the condition being treated. Consultations may differ in manner from one therapist to another, but detailed case notes will be taken, including all relevant treatments, both past and current, and any other information that it is felt might be relevant to the problem. Each session will last from approximately 30 minutes to one hour. It is not usual for hypnosis to be used at the first consultation, although a patient's reaction to it may be assessed. The patient should also be fully informed as to the content of each session and should be prepared to cooperate with the therapist in any discussion as to the object and aim of the treatment.

To induce a trance, the hypnotherapist will ask a patient to concentrate his or her attention on a fixed object or something that is moving slowly, and this will encourage the patient to become drowsy. While the patient is at this level of consciousness, the therapist is able to encourage him or her to view any problem more positively, to realize what he or she can achieve and also to understand any events in his or her past history and how he or she might be likely to react in the future. It is quite unusual for a patient actually to go to sleep after he or she has been in a trance. Should this happen, it demonstrates only that the person has not had sufficient sleep and is merely tired. It is quite commonplace for a patient to use hypnosis on himself or herself after the ailment or problem, such as insomnia or asthma, has been resolved. With a little daily practice, he or she will be able to help himself or herself considerably should the need arise for further or frequent treatment. To assist the patient, a therapist might provide a prerecorded tape of the known commencement of each session that leads up to the trance. The following example shows how a person could overcome a fear of flying.

At the first visit to the hypnotherapist, once in a trance, the patient was told to imagine travelling and arriving at an airport. At the second and subsequent visits, the person gradually imagined the stages of boarding an aeroplane, going on a very short flight and finally travelling to a different country. To help the patient afterwards, a recording of the consultations was made and this could be played in the home whenever required. The treatment proved to be completely successful, with the patient being able to further his career by flying overseas frequently.

It is considered advisable to consult a hypnotherapist who is qualified as a general practitioner too, since should there be any specific disease present it will be recognized as such. Not all doctors are convinced that there is a scientific foundation for hypnosis, but for those who are also qualified hypnotherapists, the practice is incorporated with the usual treatments available. Once a person is in a trance and past events have been brought to mind, other bodily functions, such as brain activity and the pulse rate, will react as if the event were actually happening. One interesting effect is when a person in a trance imagines himself or herself to be a very young baby. If the foot is stroked gently on the underneath, the reflex action is for the toes to curl upwards. This is the reflex response of a baby under six months old, after which the toes no longer curl upwards but downwards. This demonstrates how the person actually regresses to being very young and with the reflex actions applicable to that age.

Although aware of the existence of this sort of evidence, doubt has been expressed by some doctors that people are actually put into a trance. They tend to believe that there are different sorts of consciousness, with the one related to reality ceasing to work and another level taking control that is associated more with the imaginative and perceptive part of the mind. When fully conscious, the normal reaction would be to reject any thoughts or suggestions placed while under the influence of hypnosis. Concern has been expressed that a patient's memories of past events have been slightly modified or altered in some way to become what the patient or therapist would want them to be. Although these uncertainties about the trance state do exist, it is still recognized that hypnotherapy provides relief from pain without the use of drugs and is valuable in the treatment of various psychosomatic disorders. Problems caused by stress and anxiety can also be treated successfully.

Kinesiology

Kinesiology is a method of maintaining health by ensuring that all muscles are functioning correctly. It is believed that each muscle is connected with a specific part
of the body, such as the digestive system, circulation of
the blood and specific organs, and if a muscle is not functioning correctly this will cause a problem in its related
part of the body. The word is derived from *kinesis*, which
is Greek for 'motion'. Kinesiology originated in 1964 and
was developed by an American chiropractor named
George Goodheart, who realized that while he was treating a patient for severe pain in the leg by massaging a particular muscle in the upper leg, the pain experienced by
the patient eased and the muscle was strengthened. Although he used the same method on different muscles, the
results were not the same. Previous research done by an
osteopath named Dr Chapman, in the 1900s, indicated
that there were certain 'pressure points' in the body that
were connected with particular muscles and if these were
massaged, lymph would be able to flow more freely
through the body. Using these pressure points, Chapman
found which point was connected to each particular muscle and realized why, when he had massaged a patient's
upper leg muscle, the pain had lessened. The pressure
point for that leg muscle was the only one that was situ-

ated above the actual muscle—all the other points were
not close to the part of the body with which they were
connected.

In the 1930s it was claimed that there were similar
pressure points located on the skull and, by exerting a
light pressure on these, the flow of blood to their related
organs could be assisted. Goodheart tested this claim,
which originated from an osteopath called Terence
Bennett, and discovered that after only fingertip pressure
for a matter of seconds, it improved the strength of a particular muscle. After some time he was able to locate 16
points on the head, the back of the knee, and by the breastbone, which were all allied to groups of important muscles. Goodheart was surprised that so little force applied
on the pressure point could have such an effect on the
muscle, so to further his studies he then applied himself to
acupuncture. In this form of healing use is also made of
certain points located over the body but that run along
specific paths known as meridians. After further study,
Goodheart came to the conclusion that the meridians
could be used for both muscles and organs. The invisible
paths used in kinesiology are exactly the same as the ones
for acupuncture.

A kinesiologist will examine a patient and try to discover whether there is any lack of energy, physical disorder or inadequate nutrition causing problems. Once any
troublesome areas have been located, the practitioner will
use only a light massage on the relevant pressure points
(which, as mentioned, are generally not close to their associated muscle). For example, the edge of the rib cage is

where the pressure points for the muscles of the upper leg are situated. In kinesiology it is maintained that the use of pressure points is effective because the flow of blood to muscles is stimulated and therefore a good supply of lymph is generated too. Lymph is a watery fluid that takes toxins from the tissues, and if muscles receive a good supply of both lymph and blood they should function efficiently. As in acupuncture, it is maintained that there is an unseen flow of energy that runs through the body, and if this is disrupted for any reason, such as a person being ill or suffering from stress, then the body will weaken because of insufficient energy being produced. The way in which a kinesiologist assesses the general health of a patient is by testing the strength of the muscles, as this will provide information on the flow of energy. It is claimed that by finding any imbalance and correcting it, kinesiology can be used as a preventive therapy. If there is a lack of minerals and vitamins in the body or trouble with the digestive system, it is claimed that these are able to be diagnosed by the use of kinesiology. If a person is feeling 'below par' and constantly tired, it is believed that these conditions are aggravated by a sluggish flow of the internal body fluids, such as the circulation of blood. Kinesiologists can treat the disorder by stimulating the flow of lymph and blood by massaging the pressure points.

Although it is claimed that kinesiology can be of help to all people, it is widely known for the treatment of people suffering from food allergies or those who are sensitive to some foods. It is believed that the chemicals and nutrients contained in food cause various reactions in the

body, and if a particular food has the effect of making
muscles weak, then it would be concluded that a person
has an allergy to it. Allergic reactions can cause other
problems such as headaches, tension, colds, tiredness and a
general susceptibility to acquiring any passing infections.

There are two simple tests that can easily be tried at
home to determine if there is any sensitivity or allergy to
certain foods. This is done by testing the strength of a
strong muscle in the chest. To carry this out the person being tested will need the help of a partner. There is no need
to exert real force at any time, just use the minimum
amount needed to be firm but gentle. To test the chest
muscle, sit erect, holding the left arm straight out at right
angles to the body. The elbow should be facing outwards
and the fingers and thumb drooping towards the table.
The partner will then place his or her right hand on the
person's nearest shoulder (the right) and the two fingers
only on the area around the left wrist. A gentle downward
pressure is then exerted by the partner on the wrist of the
person who will try to maintain the level of the arm, while
breathing in a normal fashion. This downward pressure
should be exerted for approximately five seconds. If the
person was able to resist the downwards pressure and the
muscle felt quite firm, then the allergy test can be tried. If
this was not the case, however, and the person was unable
to keep the arm level, the muscle would not be suitable for
use in the subsequent test. It would therefore be advisable
to use another muscle, such as one in the arm. To do this,
place an arm straight down at the side of the body with the
palm of the hands facing outwards. The partner will then

use the same amount of pressure to try to move the arm outwards, again for a similar amount of time. If the person is unable to keep the arm in the same position, then it would be advisable to get in touch with a trained kinesiologist.

To undertake the allergy test, hold the left arm in the same way as for testing the muscle. If, for example, the food that is suspected of causing an allergy is chocolate, a small piece of this should be put just in the mouth—there is no need for it to be eaten. This time, as well as applying the pressure on the wrist as before, the partner should put his or her first two digits of the left hand below the person's right ear. Once again, the person tries to resist the

figure 47: allergy test

downwards force and, if successful, it is claimed that there is no sensitivity or allergy connected with that food. If this does not happen, however, and the arm is pushed downwards or even feels slightly weak, then kinesiology would suggest that this food, if eaten at all, should never be consumed in any great amount (figure 47).

It is claimed that the use of kinesiology can be of benefit to people who suffer from irrational fears or phobias. An example of this is the recommendation that the bone below the eye, just level with the pupil, is softly tapped. Neck and back pain can be treated without any manipulation of joints, and some of the methods can be learnt by patients for use at home. An example of this for the alleviation of back pain is for a patient to massage the muscle situated on the inside of the thigh. This is said to be of benefit for any muscles that are weak as they are the reason for a painful back.

A number of other practitioners, such as homoeopaths, herbalists and osteopaths, make use of kinesiology, so if there is a problem connected with the ligaments, muscles or bones it may be advisable to contact a chiropractor or osteopath who is also qualified in kinesiology. If the problem is of a more emotional or mental nature, then it might be best to select a counsellor or psychotherapist who also practises kinesiology. It is important always to use a fully qualified practitioner, and the relevant association should be contacted for information. At the first consultation, detailed questions will be asked concerning the medical history, followed by the therapist checking the muscles' ability to function effectively. For instance, a slight pressure

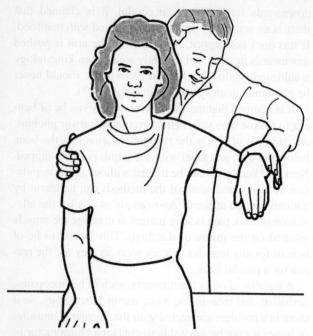

figure 48: testing for weakness in a shoulder muscle

will be exerted on a leg or arm while the patient holds it in
a certain way. The patient's ability to maintain that position against the pressure is noted and if the patient is unable to do so, then the therapist will find the reason why
by further examination. Once the areas in need of 're-bal-
ancing' have been identified, the therapist will use the relevant pressure points to correct matters. It is believed that
if some of the points are painful or sore to the touch, this

is because there has been an accumulation of toxins in the tissues, and these toxins stop the impulses between muscles and the brain. If this is the case, the muscle is unable to relax properly and can cause problems in areas such as the neck and shoulders.

There are ways of identifying any possible problems. For example, if there is any weakness in the shoulder muscle it may be that there is some problem connected with the lungs. To test for this, the patient sits upright with one arm raised to slightly below shoulder level and the other arm lower and out to the front. The therapist grasps the patient's upper arm and presses gently downwards on the raised arm at the elbow. If the muscle is functioning correctly then this downwards force should not be allowed to move the arm lower (figure 48). If the patient is suffering from pain in the back, the probable cause lies with weak muscles in the stomach. To test for this, the patient sits on the floor with the knees raised, the arms crossed on the chest and then he or she leans backwards. The therapist checks the stomach muscles' efficiency by pushing gently backwards on the patient's crossed arms. If all is well the patient should be able to maintain the position and not lean back any further (figure 49).

After treatment by massage of the pressure points, there may well be some tenderness experienced for one or two days as the toxins in the tissues dissipate gradually. However, there should be an overall feeling of an improvement in health and in particular with the problem that was being treated.

Although there has been an increase in the use of

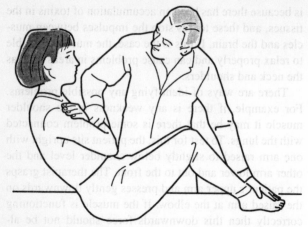

figure 49: testing for weak stomach muscles

kinesiology by doctors to help discover the cause of an ailment, there has been little scientific research carried out. Therefore, the majority of doctors using conventional medicine do not believe that the flow of electrical energy present in the body can be changed by the use of massage or similar methods.

Massage

As long ago as 3000 BC, massage was used as a therapy in the Far East, making it one of the oldest treatments used by humankind. In 5 BC in ancient Greece, Hippocrates recommended that to maintain health a massage using oils should be taken daily after a perfumed bath. The physicians there were well used to treating people who suffered from pain and stiffness in the joints.

Massage increased in popularity when Per Henrik Ling, a Swedish athlete, created the basis for what is now known as Swedish massage. This occurred in the 19th century, and massage became ever more popular in Europe from that time. Oil is used for all the different sorts of massage. Swedish massage is a combination of relaxing effects and exercises that work on the joints and muscles, but it is still based on the form that was practised in ancient times. More recently, a work was published by George Downing in the 1970s called *The Massage Book*, and this introduced a new concept in the overall technique of massage. He put forward the idea that the whole person's state should be assessed by the therapist and not solely his or her physical side. The emotional and mental states should be part of the overall picture. Also combined in his form of massage were the methods used in reflexology and shiatsu, and this was known as therapeutic massage. The aim of this is to use relaxation, stimulation and invigoration in turn to promote the highest possible level of health.

This massage is commonly used to induce general relaxation, so that any tension or strain experienced in the rush of daily life can be eased and eliminated. It is found to be very effective, working on the mind as well as the body. It can be used to treat people with hypertension (high blood pressure), sinusitis, headaches, insomnia and hyperactivity, and it can include people who suffer from heart ailments or circulatory disorders. At the physical level, massage is intended to help the body make use of food and to eliminate the waste materials, as well as stimulating the nervous and muscular system and the circulation of blood. Neck and back pain are conditions from which many people suffer, particularly if they have not been sitting correctly, such as in a slightly stooped position with their shoulders rounded. People whose day-to-day work involves a great deal of physical activity, such as dancers and athletes, can also derive a great deal of benefit from the use of massage. Stiffness can be a problem that they have after training or working, and this is relieved by encouraging the toxins that gather in the muscles to disperse. Massage promotes a feeling of calmness and serenity, and this is particularly beneficial to people who frequently suffer from bouts of depression or anxiety. Once the worry and depression have been dispelled, people are able to deal with their problems much more effectively and, being able to do so, will boost their self-confidence.

In hospitals, massage has been used to ease pain and

discomfort experienced by patients. It is also of benefit to people who are bedridden since the flow of blood to the muscles is stimulated, and it has also been used for those who have suffered a heart attack and has helped their recovery. A more recent development has been the use of massage for cancer patients who are suffering from the aftereffects of treatment of the disease, such as chemotherapy, as well as the discomfort the disease itself causes. Indeed, there are few conditions in which it is not recommended. It should not be used, however, when people are suffering from inflammation of the veins (phlebitis), varicose veins, thrombosis (clots in the blood) or if they have a raised temperature such as occurs during a fever. It is then advisable to contact a doctor before using massage. Doctors may be able to recommend a qualified therapist, a health centre may be able to help, or the relevant professional body can be contacted.

It is quite usual nowadays for a masseur or masseuse to combine treatment with the use of other methods, such as aromatherapy, acupuncture or reflexology. Massage can be divided into four basic forms, and these are known as *percussion* (also known as drumming), *friction* (also called pressure), *effleurage* (also called stroking) and *petrissage* (also called kneading). These four methods can be practised alone or in combination for maximum benefit to the patient. Massage is a therapy in which both parties derive an overall feeling of wellbeing—the therapist by the skilful use of the hands to impart the relaxation, and the patient through the therapy being administered.

Percussion is also called tapotement, as it is derived

from *tapoter*, a French word that means 'to drum', as of the fingers on a surface. As would be expected from its name, percussion is generally done with the edge of the hand with a quick, chopping movement, although the strokes are not hard. This type of movement would be used on places like the buttocks, thighs, waist or shoulders where there is a wide expanse of flesh (figure 50).

Friction is often used on dancers and athletes who experience problems with damaged ligaments or tendons. This is because the flow of blood is stimulated and the movement of joints is improved. Friction can be performed with the base of the hand, some fingers, or the upper part of the thumb. It is not advisable to use this method on parts of the body that have been injured in some way, for example where there is bruising (figure 51).

Effleurage is performed in a slow, controlled manner, using both hands together with a small space between the thumbs. If the therapist wishes to use only light pressure, he or she will use the palms of the hands or the tips of the fingers, while for increased pressure the knuckles or thumbs will be used (figure 52).

Petrissage employs a kneading and squeezing action on parts of a muscle. As the therapist works across each section, an area of flesh is grasped and squeezed, and this action will stimulates the flow of blood and enables tensed muscles to relax. People such as athletes can have an accumulation of lactic acid in certain muscles, and this is the reason why cramp occurs. Parts of the body on which this method is practised are along the stomach and around the waist (figure 53).

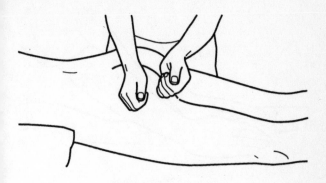

figure 50: percussion

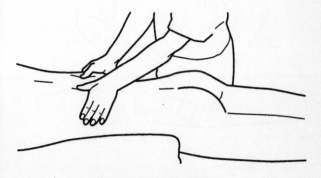

figure 51: friction

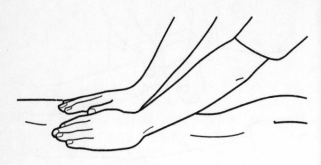

figure 52: effleurage

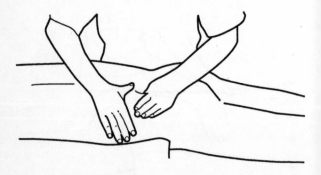

figure 53: petrissage

A session may be undertaken in the patient's home if preferred, or he or she can attend a masseur or masseuse at his or her clinic. At each session the client will undress, leaving on only pants or briefs, and will lie on a firm, comfortable surface, such as a table that is designed especially for massage. The massage that follows normally lasts from 20 minutes to one hour. Women in labour have found that the pain experienced during childbirth can be eased if massage is performed on the buttocks and back. The massage eases the build-up of tension in the muscles, encouraging relaxation and easing labour pains. It can be done by either a partner, nurse or a therapist and is said to be more effective on women who had previously experienced the benefits and reassurance of massage.

For anyone who is competent and wishes to provide some simple massage for a partner, there are some basic rules that should be taken into account. The room should be warm and peaceful. The surface on which the person lies should be quite comfortable but firm. A futon (a quilted Japanese mattress) can be used, and to relieve the upper part of the body from any possible discomfort, a pillow should be placed underneath the torso. Any pressure that may be exerted on the feet can be dispelled by the use of a rolled-up towel or similar placed beneath the ankles. Both people should be in the right frame of mind to benefit from the massage, and to this end soft music can be played. All the movements of the hand should be of a continuous nature with no break or gap between them. It is suggested that the masseur or masseuse always has one hand placed on the recipient. Vegetable oil (about one teaspoonful) is suitable but should not be poured straight on to the person. It should be spread over the hands by rubbing, which will also warm it sufficiently for use. Should the masseur or masseuse become out of breath, he or she should stop for a rest, all the while retaining a hand on the person. There is no need to wear jewellery of any sort, and comfortable clothes are the most suitable.

Massage of the head and face begins with the forehead, which should be massaged using the thumbs. This is done by stroking them outwards from the centre, across the forehead. This can also be repeated for the cheeks. The jawline can then be squeezed along its full extent using the thumb and forefinger in a circular motion (figure 54). The head can be massaged by all the fingers using a circular motion. While the person's head is being supported at

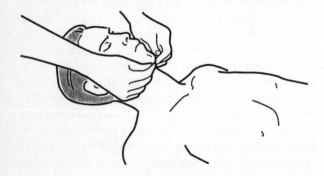

figure 54: massage of head and face

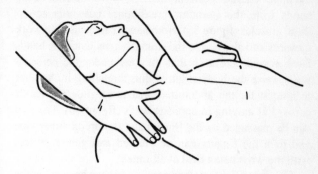

figure 55: massage of upper chest

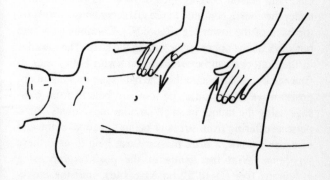

figure 56: massage of abdominal area

the side, the muscles in the neck can be gently massaged, beginning at the top and moving downwards. To exercise the upper chest or pectoral muscles, move the base of the hands from the sternum (breastbone) outwards across these muscles (figure 55). Both hands can be used to work upwards and also across the stomach area. Once the hands have moved across so that they are under the person's waist, raise the body slightly, thus stretching it. Another technique for the abdominal area is to glide the hands across but moving in opposite ways (figure 56). The arm can be massaged by the fingers and thumb on either side and then the fingers can be pressed and gently pulled, with the wrist being held at all times.

Effleurage (as described previously) can be used on the upper leg as far up as the hip on the outside of the leg. Once the person is lying face downwards (with support under the chest), continue to use effleurage movements on the back of the lower leg (figure 57). Continue as before but work on the upper leg, avoiding the knee. The muscles in the buttocks can be worked upon with both hands to squeeze but making sure that the hands are moving in opposite ways (figure 58). The foot will benefit from massage using the thumb in small circular movements. For a person suffering from stress or being 'on edge' at the end of a day's work, a back massage can help to ease these problems. With the hands in the position for using effleurage (*see* figure 52 on page 146), start the movements at the lowest part of the back and work up and then sideways to the shoulders. The pressure used should be kept up, but as soon as the hands move downwards it

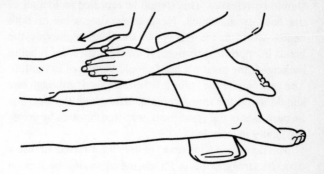

figure 57: effleurage on the lower legs

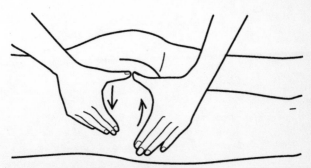

figure 58: effleurage on the buttocks

should be released. This should be repeated so that all of the back is massaged. Next, using the palms of both hands, work on the top of the shoulder by moving the hands in opposite directions. If the right shoulder is being massaged, the person's head should be turned to the left. The area beside the spine can be massaged, although one should avoid the spinal column. Using both thumbs, one on each side of the spine itself, massage this area by pressing gently in a circle.

Massage has a wide range of uses for a variety of disorders. Its strengths lie in the easing of strain and tension and inducing relaxation and serenity, plus the physical contact of the therapist. Although doctors make use of this therapy in conjunction with orthodox medicine, it is not to be regarded as a cure for disease in itself, and serious problems could occur if this were to be the case.

Osteopathy

This is a therapy that aims to pinpoint and treat any problems that are of a mechanical nature. The body's frame consists of the skeleton, muscles, joints and ligaments, and all movements or activities such as running, swimming, eating, speaking and walking depend upon it. The practice of osteopathy was originated by Dr Andrew Still (1828–1917). He was an American doctor who came to believe that it would be safer to encourage the body to heal itself rather than use the drugs that were then available and that were not always safe. He regarded the body from an engineer's point of view, and the combination of this and his medical experience of anatomy led him to believe that ailments and disorders could occur when the bones or joints no longer functioned in harmony. He believed that manipulation was the cure for the problem. Although his ideas provoked a great deal of opposition from the American medical profession at first, they slowly came to be accepted. The bulk of scientific research has been done in America with a number of medical schools of osteopathy being established. Dr Martin Littlejohn, who was a pupil of Dr Still, brought the practice of osteopathy to the UK around 1900, with the first school being founded in London in 1917.

Problems that prevent the body from working correctly

or that create pain can be caused by an injury or stress. This can result in what is known as a tension headache since the stress experienced causes a contraction in muscles. These are situated at the back of the neck at the base of the skull, and relief can be obtained by the use of massage. In osteopathy, it is believed that if the basic framework of the body is undamaged, then all physical activities can be accomplished efficiently and without causing any problems. The majority of an osteopath's patients suffer from disorders of the spine that result in pain in the lower part of the back and the neck. A great deal of pressure is exerted on the spinal column, and especially on the cartilage between the individual vertebrae. This is a constant pressure because of the effects of gravity merely by standing. If a person stands incorrectly, with stooped shoulders, this will exacerbate any problems or perhaps initiate one. The joints and framework of the body are manipulated and massaged where necessary so that the usual action is regained.

Athletes or dancers can receive injuries to muscles or joints, such as the ankle, hip, wrist or elbow, and they too can benefit from treatment by osteopathy. Pain in the lower back can be experienced by pregnant women who may stand in a different way because of their increasing weight, and if this is the case, osteopathy can often ease matters considerably. To find a fully qualified osteopath, it is advisable to contact the relevant professional body, or the GP may be able to help.

At the first visit to an osteopath, he or she will need to know the complete history of any problems experienced, how they first occurred, and what eases or aggravates matters. A patient's case history and any form of therapy that is currently in use will all be of relevance to the practitioner. A thorough examination will then take place, with the patient being observed as to how they sit, stand or lie down and also the manner in which the body is bent to the side, back or front. As each movement takes place, the osteopath is able to take note of the extent and ability of the joint to function. The practitioner will also feel the muscles, soft tissues and ligaments to detect if there is any tension present. While examining the body, the osteopath will note any problems that are present and, as an aid to diagnosis, may also check reflexes, such as the knee-jerk reflex. If a patient has been involved in an accident, X-rays can be checked to determine the extent of any problem. It is possible that a disorder would not benefit from treatment by osteopathy, and the patient would be advised accordingly. If this is not the case, treatment can begin with the chosen course of therapy. There is no set number of consultations necessary, as this will depend on the nature of the problem and also for how long it has been apparent. It is possible that a severe disorder that has arisen suddenly can be alleviated at once. The osteopath is likely to recommend a number of things, so that patients can help themselves between treatments. Techniques such as learning to relax, how to stand and sit correctly and additional exercises can be suggested by the osteopath. Patients generally find that each consultation is quite pleasant, and they feel much more relaxed and calm afterwards. The length of each session can vary, but it is generally in the region of half an hour. As the osteopath gently manipulates the joint, any tenseness present in the muscles will be lessened and its ability to work correctly and to its maximum extent also improved. It is this manipulation that can cause a clicking noise to be heard. As well as manipulation, other methods such as massage can be used to good effect. Muscles can be freed from tension if the tissue is massaged, and this will also stimulate the flow of blood. In some cases, the patient may experience a temporary deterioration once treatment has begun, and this is more likely to occur if the ailment has existed for quite some time.

People who have to spend a lot of their time driving are susceptible to a number of problems related to the manner in which they are sitting. If the position is incorrect they can suffer from tension headaches, pain in the back and the shoulders, and the neck can feel stiff. There are a number of ways in which these problems can be remedied, such as holding the wheel in the approved manner (at roughly 'ten to two' on the dial of a clock). The arms should not be held out straight and stiff, but should feel relaxed, with the arms bent at the elbow. In order that the driver can maintain a position in which the back and neck feel comfortable, the seat should be moved so that it is tilting backwards a little, although it should not be so far away that the pedals are not easily reached. The legs should not be held straight out, and if the pedals are the correct distance away, the knees should be bent a little and feel quite comfortable. It is also important to sit erect and not slump in the seat. The driver's rear should be posi-

tioned right at the back of the seat, and this should be
checked each time before using the vehicle. It is also important that there is adequate vision from the mirror so its
position should be altered if necessary. If the driver already has a back problem, then it is a simple matter to provide support for the lower part of the back. If this is done,
it should prevent strain on the shoulders and backbone.
While driving, the person should make a conscious effort
to ensure that the shoulders are not tensed but held in a
relaxed way. Another point to remember is that the chin
should not be stuck out but kept in, otherwise the neck
muscles will become tense and painful. Drivers can perform some beneficial exercises while waiting in a queue
of traffic. To stretch the neck muscles, put the chin right
down on to the chest and then relax. This stretching exercise should be done several times. Another exercise can
also be done at the same time as driving and will have a
positive effect on the flow of blood to the legs and also
will improve how a person is seated. It is simply done by
contraction and relaxation of the muscles in the stomach.
Another exercise involves raising the shoulders upwards
and then moving them backwards in a circular motion.
The head should also be inclined forward a little. This
should also be done several times to gain the maximum
effect.

Figures 59 and 60 illustrate an example of diagnosis
and treatment by manipulation in which the osteopath ex-
amines a knee that has been injured. To determine the extent of the problem, the examination will be detailed and
previous accidents or any other relevant details will be re-

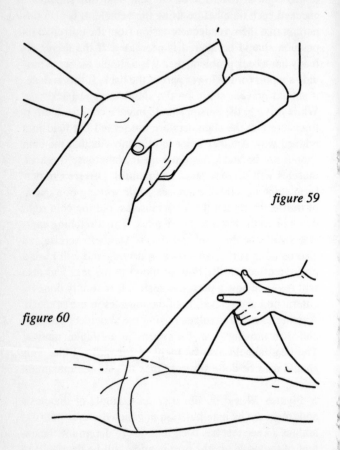

figure 59

figure 60

quested. If the practitioner concludes that osteopathy will
be of benefit to the patient, the joint will be manipulated
so that it is able to function correctly and the manipulation
will also have the effect of relaxing the muscles that have
become tensed due to the injury.

Another form of therapy, which is known as cranial osteopathy, can be used for patients suffering from pain in
the face or head. This is effected by the osteopath using
slight pressure on these areas including the upper part of
the neck. If there is any tautness or tenseness present the
position is maintained while the problem improves. It is
now quite common practice for doctors to recommend
some patients to use osteopathy and some general practitioners use the therapy themselves after receiving training. Although its benefits are generally accepted for problems of a mechanical nature, doctors believe it is vital that
they first decide upon what is wrong before any possible
use can be made of osteopathy.

Polarity Therapy

This is a therapy devised by Dr Randolph Stone (1890–1983), that amalgamates other healing therapies from both East and West. Dr Stone studied many of these therapies, including yoga and acupuncture, and he was also trained to practise osteopathy and chiropractic, among others. He began to search for a cure to the problem that he experienced with some of his patients when, although their disorder had been cured by the use of manipulation, they subsequently became unwell. Through his studies of Eastern therapies, he accepted the fundamental belief that a form of energy flows along certain channels in the body and that to keep good health the flow must be maintained. In India this energy is referred to as *prana* and in China it is called *chi* or *qi*. The Western equivalent of this would probably be called a person's soul or spirit. It is believed that ailments occur when this flow of energy is blocked or is out of balance, and this could happen for different reasons, such as tension or stress, disturbances in the mind or unhealthy eating patterns. This energy is purported to be the controlling factor in a person's whole life and therefore affect the mind and body at all levels. It is believed that once the flow of energy had been restored to normal, the ailment will disappear and not recur.

Dr Stone's polarity therapy states that there are three types of relationships, known as *neutral*, *positive* and *negative*, to be maintained between various areas in the body and five centres of energy. These centres originate from a very old belief held in India that each centre is held to have an effect on a related part of the body. The centres are known as *ether* (controlling the ears and throat), *earth* (controlling the rectum and bladder), *fire* (controlling the stomach and bowels), *water* (controlling the pelvis and glands), and *air* (controlling the circulation and breathing). The therapy's aim is to maintain a balance and harmony between all these various points, and Dr Stone slowly developed four procedures to do this. They are the use of *diet*, *stretching exercises*, *touch and manipulation*, and mental attitude, that is, contemplation allied with a positive view of life. In order that the body is cleansed from a build-up of toxins caused by unhealthy eating and environmental pollution, the person will eat only fresh vegetables, fruit juices and fresh fruit. The length of time for this diet will vary reflecting the degree of cleansing required, but it is unlikely to be longer than a fortnight. Also available is a special drink that consists of lemon juice, olive oil, garlic and ginger. After the cleansing is complete, there is another diet to be followed that is said to promote and increase health, and finally one to ensure that the body maintains its level of good health.

Various positions may be adopted for the *stretching exercises*, such as on the floor with the legs crossed (figure 61), or squatting, or sitting with the hands held at the back of the head. It is believed that these exercises free the channels that carry the body's energy and strengthen the sinews, muscles, ligaments and spine. As a way of releas-

figure 61: cross-legged position

ing any stress or tension, the person would be requested to shout out loud at the same time as exercising. For the first exercise, the person can sit on the floor cross-legged with the right hand taking hold of the left ankle and with the left hand holding the right ankle. The eyes should then be shut and the mind relaxed and quiet.

For the squatting exercise, once in this position, clasp the hands out in front for balance and then move backwards and forwards and also circle. For people unable to balance in this position, a small book or similar item put under the heels should help (figure 62).

For a slight change in the basic squatting position, bend the head forward and place the hands at the back of the

figure 62: squatting position

neck so that the head and arms are between the knees. Relax the arms a little so that they drop forward slightly and thus the backbone is stretched (figure 63).

Another variation is to hold the hands behind the neck whilst squatting and push the elbows and shoulder blades backwards and inwards. Any tension or stress can be relieved by shouting at the same time as breathing deeply.

Another exercise in which stress can be eased by shouting is known as the *wood-chopper*. This is a fairly simple one to perform, and it entails standing with the feet apart and the knees bent. The hands should be clasped above the head as if about to chop some wood and the arms brought down together in a swinging action ending

figure 63: a variation on the squatting position

with the arms as far between the legs as possible. As the hands are being swung downwards, the person should shout, so that any tension is relieved. This action can be repeated quite frequently as long as there is no discomfort (figures 64 and 65).

Touch and manipulation are used by the therapist to detect any stoppages in the flow of energy along the channels, which are believed to be the reason for disorders. It is said that by the use of pressure, of which there are three sorts, the therapist is able to restore the flow of energy.

Neutral pressure is gentle and calming and only the tips of the fingers are used.

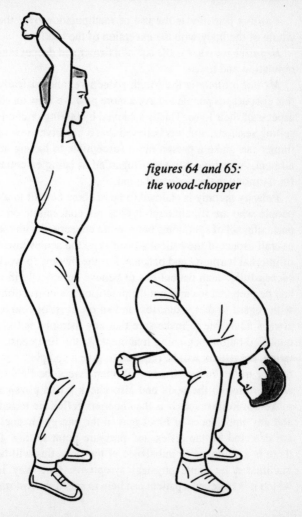

figures 64 and 65:
the wood-chopper

Positive pressure is the use of manipulation over the whole of the body with the exception of the head.

Negative pressure is the use of a firmer and deeper manipulation and touch.

Mental attitude is the fourth procedure, and basically this encourages people to have a more positive view on all aspects of their lives. This is achieved by talking or counselling sessions, and it is believed that a negative view of things can make a person more susceptible to having an ailment. A positive attitude is regarded as being essential for harmony in the body and mind.

Polarity therapy is claimed to be of some benefit to all people who are ill, although it does not concentrate on a particular set of symptoms but is more concerned with the overall aspect of the patient's health and the achievement of internal harmony and balance. For the therapy to work successfully, each patient has to believe completely in it and be prepared to carry out the practitioner's instructions with regard to diet, exercises, and so on. It is, of course, always advisable to make sure that any therapist is fully qualified before beginning treatment. At the first consultation, the patient will be required to give a complete case history to the therapist, who will then assess the flow of energy through the body and also check on its physical make-up. Reflexes such as the knee-jerk reflex are tested, and any imbalances or blockages in the energy channels are detected by the reflex and pressure point testing. If there is a stoppage or imbalance of the flow, this will be manifested by some physical symptoms. One way in which it is believed a patient can help to speed the restoration of health is by remembering and concentrating on any thoughts, feelings or pictures in the 'mind's eye' that happen while a particular area is being treated. The patient should also have knowledge of the body's ability to heal itself. If a patient is receiving treatment for a painful knee joint, for example, he or she should focus attention on that part of the body while being receptive to any feelings that occur. It is believed that if the patient is aware of the overall condition, as a complete person and not just the physical aspect, this will encourage restoration of health. It is possible that a patient will need to keep details of all food consumed to enable the practitioner to detect any harmful effects and a 'fruit and vegetable' diet may be advised (as described previously). It may be that the patient has some habit, view or manner of life that is not considered conducive to good health. If this is the case, the patient would be able to take advantage of a counselling service in order to help make a change. Other alternative therapies, such as the use of herbal medicine, may be used to effect a cure.

Polarity therapy has much in common with other Eastern remedies that have the common themes of contemplation, exercise, touch or pressure, and diet that can give much improvement. However, it is recommended that an accurate medical analysis of any condition is found in the first instance.

Yoga

From its Indian origins as far back as 4000 years ago, yoga has been continually practised, but it is only in the present century that its use has become more widespread. Yoga has an effect on the whole person, combining the physical, mental and spiritual sides. The word 'yoga' is derived from a Sanskrit word that means 'yoke' or 'union' and thus reflects on the practices of yoga being total in effect. For many hundreds of years in India only a select few, such as philosophers and like-minded people with their disciples, followed the way of life that yoga dictated. The leaders were known as 'yogis', and it was they who taught their followers by passing on their accumulated knowledge. These small groups of people did not live with the people in the villages but dwelt in caves or woods, or sometimes a yogi would live like a hermit. Yoga has had quite far-reaching effects over many hundreds of years in India. There is a form of traditional healing known as Ayurvedic medicine in which some basic exercises from yoga are used as part of the treatment.

The basics of yoga were defined by a yogi called Patanjali, who lived about 300 BC. He was a very well-respected teacher and commanded great influence at that time, and his classification is one that is used now. He established the fact of yoga being separated into eight dif-

ferent parts. The first two concern a person's lifestyle,
which should be serene, with the days spent in contemplation, study, in maintaining cleanliness and living very
simply and at peace with others. Anything that involves
avarice or greed, etc, or is harmful to others has to be
avoided. The third and fourth parts are concerned with
physical matters and list a number of exercises designed
to promote peace and infuse energy into both the mind
and body. The remaining four sections are concerned with
the advancement of a person's soul or spirit and mental
faculties by being able to isolate himself or herself from
outside worries and normal life, contemplation and broad-
ening mental faculties with the ultimate knowledge
known as *somadhi*. This is a complete change mentally,
which gives final realization of existence. Much more recently, yoga became available in India to everyone, in
complete contrast to centuries ago. Doctors and teachers
taught yoga, and it is now the rule that all schoolchildren
have lessons in some of the exercises.

Nowadays, the practice of yoga is not restricted to India alone, with millions of people worldwide being followers. There are actually five different types of yoga:
raja, *jnana*, *karma*, *bakti*, and *hatha*. It is the last system
that is known in the West and it involves the use of exercises and positions. The other methods concentrate on
matters such as control over the mind, appreciation and
intelligence or a morally correct way of life. These other
methods are regarded as being of equal importance by the
person completely committed to yoga as a way of life. Although people may have little or no spiritual feeling, the

basic belief of yoga is the importance of mental attitudes in establishing the physical improvements from exercise. Because of media coverage of a famous violinist receiving successful treatment to a damaged shoulder by yoga, it became very popular throughout the UK. Prior to the 1960s, it was seldom practised, and only then by people who wanted to learn more of Eastern therapies or who had worked and travelled in that area.

It is a belief in yoga that the body's essence of life, or *prana*, is contained in the breath. Through a change in the way of breathing there can be a beneficial effect on the general health. If a person is in a heightened emotional condition, or similar state, this will have an effect on the breathing. Therefore, if the breathing is controlled or altered, this should promote joint feelings of peace and calm, both mentally and emotionally. There are a variety of exercises, and each promotes different types of breathing, such as the rib cage, shoulder and diaphragm. Some of the movements and stances in use were originally devised from the observation of animals, since they appeared to be adept at relaxation and moved with minimum effort. These stances, which are maintained for one or two minutes, aim to increase freedom of movement and make the person aware of the various parts of the body and any stress that may be present. They are not intended to be physically tiring or to allow the person to 'show off' in front of others. The aim is to concentrate on self-knowledge.

The following 12 stances, known as *a greeting to the sun*, have the aim of relaxing and invigorating the body and mind. As suggested by its name, it was originally done when the sun rose and when it set. Although these stances are quite safe, they should not be done by pregnant women or those having a monthly period, except with expert tuition. If a person has hypertension (high blood pressure), a hernia, clots in the blood or pain in the lower back, they are not recommended. Each exercise should follow on smoothly one after the other.

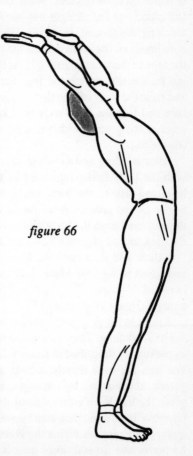

figure 66

Firstly, stand to attention, hold the palms of the hands together next to the chest with fingers upright. Then inhale and stretch the arms upright with the palms facing the ceiling and lean backwards (figure 66).

Exhale and, keeping the legs straight, place the fingers or palms on to the ground. While inhaling, bend the knees and place one leg straight out backwards, with the knee touching the ground, in a long, lunging movement. With both hands on the ground, raise the head slightly and push the hips to the front (figure 67). At the same time as holding the breath, stretch the legs out together backwards, and raise the body off the floor supported by the arms. Exhale and fold the body over bent knees so that the head touches the ground with the arms stretched out in front (figure 68).

After inhaling and exhaling once, lie face downwards with the body being supported by the hands at shoulder level and also by the toes. The stomach and hips should not be on the ground. After taking a deep breath, stretch the arms and push the body upwards with the head up and the back arched (figure 69 on page 174).

Exhale and then raise the hips upwards with the feet and hands being kept on the floor so that the body is in an inverted V-shape. The legs and back should be kept straight (figure 70 on page 175).

Revert to the position as shown in figure 68 after inhaling and exhaling. Then inhale and move into the position as previously described in figure 67, except that the opposite legs are used. Lastly, exhale and place the feet together, keeping the legs straight. Bend downwards and place the hands on either side of the feet on the floor, if possible. Inhale and then stand up straight. This whole sequence of exercises forms the greeting or salute and can be performed several times over if wished. If this is the

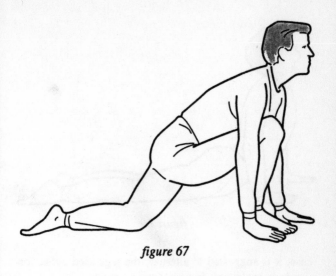

figure 67

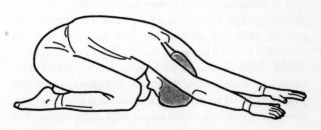

figure 68

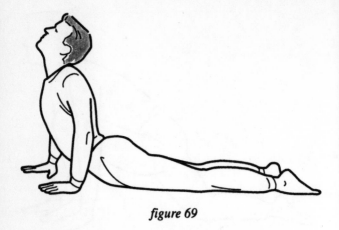

figure 69

case, it is suggested to alternate the legs used either forwards or backwards in two of the exercises.

It is recommended to follow some simple rules when
practising yoga. Firstly, use a fully qualified therapist, and
practise daily if at all possible. It is advisable to check
with a GP first if a person is undergoing a course of treatment or is on permanent medication, has some sort of in-
firmity or feels generally unwell. It is always best that
yoga is undertaken before mealtimes but if this is not possible then three hours must elapse after a large meal or an
hour after a light one. Comfortable clothes are essential,
and a folded blanket or thick rug should be placed on the
ground as the base. Before beginning yoga have a bath or
shower and repeat this afterwards to gain the maximum

figure 70

benefit. It is not advisable to do yoga if either the bowels
or bladder are full. If the person is among a group under
instruction there should be no element of competition.
Should the person have been outside on a hot and sunny
day it is not recommended that yoga is practised straight
afterwards, as feelings of sickness and dizziness may occur.

Yoga is believed to be of benefit to anyone, providing
that he or she possesses determination and patience. If a
person has certain physical limitations then these must be
taken into account with regard to their expectation, but
there is no age barrier. Teachers believe that people suffering from stress and disorder in their lives are in greater
need of a time of harmony and peace. Yoga was used in

the main to encourage health in the physical and mental states and thereby act as a preventive therapy. Tension or stress was one of the main disorders for which it was used, but nowadays it has been used for differing disorders such as hypertension (high blood pressure), bronchitis, back pain, headaches, asthma, heart disorders, premenstrual tension and an acid stomach. Trials have also been conducted to assess its potential in treating some illnesses such as multiple sclerosis, cerebral palsy, osteoporosis, rheumatoid arthritis and depression experienced after childbirth. Since the effects of tension are often shown by the tightening and contraction of muscles, the stretching exercises performed in yoga are able to release it. Also, by being aware of each muscle as it is stretched encourages the person to lose mentally any stress or problems with which he or she has been beset. Suppleness is developed by the exercises through the use of the bending and twisting actions. This will help to maintain healthy joints, particularly for people who lead rather inactive lives.

The following five stances are ideal for newcomers to yoga, although it may not be possible to do them correctly for some weeks. There should be no strain felt, and after practice some or all of them can be done in order. As mentioned previously, it is best to check with a qualified therapist if the person is an expectant mother, suffers from hypertension (high blood pressure), is overweight or is having a monthly period.

The first exercise is known as the *spinal twist*, and the person should sit on the floor with the legs outstretched.

figure 41: the bow

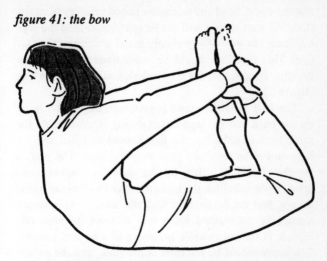

The left leg should be bent and placed over the other leg as far as possible. The person should exhale and twist the body to the left. The person's right hand should be moved towards the right foot. The person should have the body supported by placing the left hand on the ground at the back but keeping the back straight. Every time the person exhales the body should be further twisted to the left. The position should be maintained for approximately one minute and then the complete action done again, but this time turning to the right.

The *bow* entails lying face down on the ground. The knees should be bent and then raised in the direction of the head. The hands should then hold the ankles and, while inhaling, a pull should be exerted on the ankles so that the chest, head and thighs are raised up away from the floor. To start with it will not be possible to hold the legs together, but this will gradually occur with regular practice. This position should be maintained for up to ten breaths. To complete the bow, exhale and let go of the legs (figure 71).

The *half shoulder stand* begins with the person lying on the back and the legs raised during inhalation. At the same time as exhaling, the hips should be lifted and the legs moved so that they pass over the head. The body's weight should be taken by the shoulders, elbows and arms. Upon inhaling, the legs are moved so that the hands do not feel uncomfortable with the weight. This stance should be maintained for a few minutes (perhaps one minute at the start) while breathing in a normal manner. The arms should be returned to the floor, and the person should inhale while letting the body gradually return to the floor in a rolling action.

The *bridge* is again done on the floor, starting with the person lying on the back. The knees should be bent, with the legs separated a little and the arms at the side of the body. The person should then inhale and lift the torso and legs, thus forming a bridge. The fingers should then be linked under the body and the arms held straight. The person should then incline the body to each side in turn, ensuring that the shoulders stay underneath. To make the bridge a little bigger, pressure can be exerted by the arms and feet. After inhaling, the position should be maintained for a minimum of one minute and the body returned to a relaxed normal position on the floor (figure 72).

figure 72: the bridge

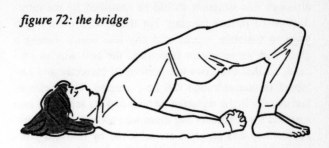

The last stance is known as the *triangle* and commences with the person standing upright with the legs apart and the arms held out at shoulder level. Extend the right foot to the side and, upon exhaling, bend over the right-hand side so that the right hand slips downwards in the direction of the ankle. There should be no forward inclination of the body at this time. As the bending action takes place, the left arm should be lifted upright with the palm of the hand to the front. This stretched position should be kept up for the minimum of a minute, with the person trying to extend the stretch as he or she exhales. After inhaling, the person should then revert to the beginning of the exercise and do it again but leaning in the opposite direction.

As previously mentioned, yoga has recently been used to treat some illnesses such as rheumatoid arthritis and if a person has such a severe disorder then a highly skilled and experienced therapist is essential. Since this form of yoga, known as therapeutic yoga, is so new there are only a limited number of suitably experienced therapists available, although this situation should be remedied by the introduction of further training. For those who wish to use yoga to maintain mental and physical health joining a class with an instructor is perhaps the best way to proceed, so that exercises are performed correctly and any lapses in concentration can be corrected. These classes last usually in the region of an hour and are separated into sessions for beginners and those who are more proficient. Proficiency and progress are achieved by frequent practice, which can be done at home between lessons. One simple exercise that helps reduce stress is quite simple to perform and does not take long. The person should lie on the floor with the arms at the side and the legs together. After inhaling, all the muscles from the toes to the thighs should be tightened in turn. As the person exhales the muscles in the stomach up to the shoulders should then be tightened, including the hands, which should be clenched. After inhaling again, the chest, throat and face muscles should be tightened as well as screwing up the face, and this should be maintained until the next breath has to be taken. All muscles should then be relaxed, the legs parted and the arms spread out comfortably with the palms facing the ceiling. The person should then totally relax with a sensation of falling through the ground.

The majority of doctors regard yoga as a type of exercise that is beneficial, although some do recommend patients to yoga practitioners. If a specific disorder is to be treated, however, it is very important that the ailment should first be seen by a doctor.

Index